First Hundred

Teviotdale Harriers Club
1889 Centenary 1989

By

JOHN L. COLTMAN

Published by the Teviotdale Harriers Centenary Committee
and
Printed by the "Hawick News," 24 High Street, Hawick
1988

TEVIOTDALE Harriers acknowledge the financial assistance received from Lyle & Scott, knitwear manufacturers, Lynnwood Road, Hawick, without whom this Centenary publication would not have been possible.

The information in this book has been updated to August 1988.

ISBN 0 9513562 0 8

Congratulatory Message from Her Majesty The Queen

ON THE OCCASION of the launch of the centenary season, Teviotdale Harriers Centenary Committee received the following message from the Queen's private secretary at Buckingham Palace:—

"The Queen sends her warm thanks to all members of the Teviotdale Harriers Club for their kind message of loyal greetings, sent on the occasion of the Centenary of the Club. Her Majesty greatly appreciated this message and sends her best wishes to you all for a most enjoyable and successful Centenary year."

THE DUKE OF BUCCLEUCH AND QUEENSBERRY, K.T.
Lord-Lieutenant of Roxburgh, Ettrick and Lauderdale
BOWHILL, SELKIRK

BEST BIRTHDAY GREETINGS and good wishes to Teviotdale Harriers on this, your 100th anniversary.

On countless occasions have I admired the dedication of your members training throughout Teviotdale and in all weathers. On many occasions your efforts have been crowned with success and I am proud of my family's long-standing association with so worthy a band of enthusiasts who excel in such an invigorating pursuit.

Author's note: The present Duke's father was a patron and honorary vice-president of the club for over 30 years. But an even earlier mention of the family's long association with the club appears in the first Minute Book. In the 1893-94 season the then Earl of Dalkeith was honorary vice-president.

RONNIE S. PRINGLE

President

TEVIOTDALE HARRIERS CLUB

ONE HUNDRED YEARS AGO, in January 1889, a new club was instituted in Hawick—Teviotdale Harriers. It was formed with the underlying objective of expanding the sporting life of Hawick, with the emphasis on cross-country running.

Since then some 20 presidents have held office and the Club has been led by 82 captains. Business men, professional men, tradesmen, knitwear and tweed workers have served the Club in these capacities. Present-day members can look back with pride on the trail that has been laid by these dedicated men and all club members of yesteryear. Each decade since January 1889 has produced personalities and champions who have established Teviotdale Harriers as one of the premier clubs in the country . . . long may it be so.

I take this opportunity to record my appreciation to all who have supported me in the preparation of events which are calculated to make the centenary celebrations memorable and worthy of such a milestone. On behalf of Teviotdale Harriers, I wish to thank the many companies and individuals who have provided sponsorship, financial and otherwise, for our celebrations. During the celebrations let us remember the founders and pioneers who had the foresight to introduce the sport in Hawick. Without them there would be no "Teviotdale Harriers Story," no triumphs to celebrate, no honours to acknowledge. My office-bearers and committee have been unstinting in their efforts on behalf of Teviotdale Harriers' One Hundreth Birthday, while the appointed Centenary Committee have been equally painstaking in the build-up to the "Big Year."

Like me, perhaps you wondered who would be knowledgeable enough and qualified to write our book entitled "First Hundred." I am especially grateful to "historian" and honorary vice-president of the Harriers Jake Coltman who undertook this onerous task. A Border sprint champion, joint club record-holder and "Hawick News" columnist "Spikes" for the past 30 years, he has compiled a comprehensive record of facts and figures, as well as many nostalgic pictures and researched data. He must have spent endless hours in his efforts to make this publication of total interest to members and supporters—past and present. It is a revealing record not only of Harriers' achievements but also of changes during the past hundred years. This publication should appeal to all who have "run with the hares and hunted with the hounds," to use a phrase associated with cross-country running in years past.

A programme of events for our centenary has been drawn up, calculated to involve every member and create excitement and keen competition, sending all concerned into the second hundred years with an injection of renewed enthusiasm . . . now let us all enjoy the celebrations to the full.

FRANK LEITHEAD

Managing Director

LYLE & SCOTT

LYLE & SCOTT was founded in Hawick only 15 years earlier than Teviotdale Harriers, so in a way it could be said we grew up together. The company has a long tradition of enterprise, linked with community spirit, much like the Harriers and both firm and club have been instrumental over the years in putting Hawick in the forefront of excellence.

A business and a club are very much alike. The management: the office-bearers, the workforce: the club members, each with its own job to do, each an integral part of the other. So what more fitting a partnership could there be to celebrate a centenary than a leading sportswear manufacturer and a leading sporting club.

We at Lyle & Scott are indeed honoured to sponsor such a publication as the Teviotdale Harriers official history book, the pages of which include the exploits of a number of our own employees who have distinguished themselves in one of Hawick's most popular sporting clubs.

Today Teviotdale Harriers are very much a way of life in the town, opening its doors to all, from children to veterans, to partake of a comradeship invaluable in our modern society.

This book—the product of a joint venture unique in Hawick—is a record and a proud one at that, of their "First Hundred." I am sure they will take the next 100 in their stride, striving for the best, just as they have done so in the decades that have gone before them.

Best wishes for the future and may all Teviotdale Harriers have a very successful centenary celebration.

ARCHY KIRKWOOD, M.P.

ROXBURGH AND BERWICKSHIRE CONSTITUENCY

HOUSE OF COMMONS

LONDON

MANY CONGRATULATIONS to Teviotdale Harriers on their Centenary; athletics not only gives enjoyment in itself but it promotes a positive outlook on life in those who take part, and encourages good health.

I wish Teviotdale every success in this special Centenary year, and for another hundred years.

H. QUINN

President

SCOTTISH CROSS-COUNTRY UNION

ON BEHALF OF ALL CLUBS affiliated to the Scottish Cross-Country Union, I wish to congratulate Teviotdale Harriers on reaching their Centenary. It is even more of an honour when that club is the third oldest in continuous existence in Scotland and currently Eastern District Champions and League title-holders — a "double" achieved for the past two seasons. Well done Teviotdale.

SANDY CAMERON

Chairman

Eastern District Committee of the S.C.C.U.

WE OFFER OUR WARMEST congratulations and best wishes to Teviotdale Harriers on being the first club in the Eastern District, and third in Scotland, to achieve 100 years of continuous existence. Teviotdale are well known for their friendliness, hospitality and real cross-country courses! We are especially happy that Hawick has been chosen to host the National Cross Country Championships in 1989, the Centenary year of the Club. Teviotdale's recent successes have included wins in the Eastern League and District Championships in 1987 and 1988. We hope that the Harriers will continue to prosper as they move into their second hundred years.

ROBERT A. CHERRIE

Chairman

Eastern District League Committee of the S.C.C.U.

IT IS A GREAT PLEASURE for me, on behalf of the Eastern District League Committee of the S.C.C.U., to extend sincere congratulations to Teviotdale Harriers on reaching their Centenary year. May I also wish Teviotdale every success for the 1988-89 cross-country season and for future years.

H. HATRICK

President

SCOTTISH BORDER A.A.A.

THE S.B.A.A.A. congratulates Teviotdale Harriers on their Centenary. Teviotdale Harriers have the distinction of being the oldest of the Scottish Borders athletic clubs. Their initiative and enthusiasm contributed greatly to the subsequent formation of other Scottish Borders Clubs and to the S.B.A.A.A. The S.B.A.A.A. wishes them continued success in the future.

J. W. McINNES

President

SCOTTISH A.A.A.

ANY CLUB reaching its Centenary is indeed an achievement. When that Centenary is reached in the Borders area it is even more of an achievement when one considers the competition for members which exists in this rugby-playing area.

On behalf of the Scottish Amateur Athletic Association I am delighted to congratulate the members and officials of Teviotdale Harriers on reaching their Centenary.

HILDA EVERETT

President

SCOTTISH WOMEN'S A.A.A.

THE SCOTTISH Women's Amateur Athletic Association extend their congratulations to Teviotdale Harriers in their Centenary year. To have survived so long in an area where athletics is not the major sport is quite an achievement and must be attributed to the officials, athletes and members of the club. Our very best wishes for success and a continuation of athletics in the Borders area.

MARJORY A. COOK

President

SCOTTISH WOMEN'S CROSS COUNTRY AND ROAD RUNNING ASSOCIATION

THE SCOTTISH Women's Cross Country and Road Running Association wishes to congratulate Teviotdale Harriers on reaching their Centenary. For many years they have been prominent in women's cross country running and our members have always enjoyed the cross country races held in Hawick.

Teviotdale women athletes have taken part in many of our Inter-League races in England and we hope that they will continue to support these races for many years to come.

I hope Teviotdale Harriers will be as successful in the next 100 years as they have been in the past.

ROXBURGH DISTRICT COUNCIL

GIDEON YELLOWLEES

Chairman

KENNETH W. CRAMOND

Chief Executive

IT IS WITH A GREAT SENSE of honour and pleasure that we send greetings on behalf of Roxburgh District Council on the occasion of your Centenary. May we congratulate you on a successful one hundred years and on the Club's record over the period.

During its existence, the Club's fortunes have, like most, fluctuated. Nevertheless, in their participation in all major National events, its members have always earned credit for its name and reputation, and brought distinction and honour to Hawick and the District, playing a significant part not only in the history of sport within the Borders but throughout the length and breadth of the United Kingdom.

This is wholly due to the combination of team spirit, skill, determination and sportsmanship, which has earned the Club respect and admiration wherever its members have competed. The office-bearers and members can be justly proud of this fine record, which continued its existence through the years of both World Conflicts. Everyone must admire that record and share that pride.

In conveying to the Club this message of congratulations, we sincerely offer you, on behalf of the District Council, its Officers and the people of Roxburgh, sincere best wishes for the next one hundred years, to which you can look forward with enthusiasm and confidence.

BORDERS REGIONAL COUNCIL

TOM HUNTER
Convener

KENNETH CLARK
Chief Executive

THIS UNIQUE OPPORTUNITY to convey best wishes for the future and congratulations on past achievements from the Regional Council to the third oldest Harriers Club in Scotland is both a privilege and a pleasure.

The presence of a strong community club to ensure a planned outlet for recreation, health and sporting talent is essential in every Border area where strong links between school sports programmes and clubs like Teviotdale Harriers can be fostered.

J. COCKBURN
Chairman
ROXBURGH DISTRICT SPORTS COUNCIL

I AM PRIVILEGED to be congratulating Teviotdale Harriers on their Centenary year and in doing so speak for all sportsmen in the District.

Teviotdale Harriers, a sporting "institution" in Hawick, has brought great credit not only to the town but to the District and Scottish Borders. They are one of the area's leading sporting clubs — long may it be so.

RAYMOND C. MIQUEL
Chairman
THE SCOTTISH SPORTS COUNCIL

TEVIOTDALE HARRIERS is one of the oldest athletic clubs in Scotland. To reach a centenary is a wonderful achievement and it reflects the dedication of generations of enthusiastic athletes and administrators. In congratulating the Club on reaching this important milestone, I am pleased to take this opportunity to wish it continued success and prosperity in the future.

MYRA TURNBULL

Provost of Hawick

IT GIVES ME great pleasure in sending you my congratulations on your publication "First Hundred," an official history of your Club and a launch pad for your Centenary celebrations in 1989. The year ahead is going to prove both busy and challenging, as I realise the hard work involved in organising such a full programme of events, but I know your efforts will be more than worthwhile. My best wishes to you all.

WHERE IT ALL BEGAN.—The Tower Hotel in the Tower Knowe as it looked in 1889 when 12 men of Hawick met in the Round Room on Thursday, 24th January, formed themselves into a club and so Teviotdale Harriers was born. The Round Room was situated to the right of the main entrance.

INTRODUCTION

This official history book is published as part of the celebrations marking the centenary of Teviotdale Harriers, thanks to the generosity of international sportswear leaders Lyle & Scott of Hawick, Scotland.

Teviotdale Harriers, formed in January, 1889, is the third oldest club in Scotland in continuous existence — the others being Clydesdale Harriers (1885) and Maryhill Harriers (1888) — and is presently one of the leading clubs in Scotland.

It is hoped that this book will revive happy memories for all runners, officials and supporters who have been, or still are, part of the comradeship of Teviotdale Harriers.

This history has involved many years of research; the selection of material used being my own responsibility. It has been the prime aim of the publication that the names of as many Teviotdale Harriers as possible, both past and present, be included in its pages but, of course, space does not allow the inclusion of everyone. A list of club trophy winners, officials and Teviotdale Harriers who have won Border track and field titles and held office in the Scottish Border Amateur Athletic Association, is contained at the back of the book.

Information on the past 30 years has come from my membership of the club during that period but the earlier years could not have been covered in such detail had I not been afforded access to the files of the "Hawick News" and for this, Teviotdale Harriers and I are indeed grateful to the proprietor, Mr Robert McNairn. Thanks also go to the late Jimmy Robson, Adie Barker and Alan Hill of the "Hawick News," Ian Rutherford and the many unknown photographers of yesteryear for the illustrations used, and R. E. Scott for his design of the official centenary logo.

Despite every effort to be accurate, some errors may occur and I beg the reader's indulgence in this matter.

JOHN L. COLTMAN,

August 1988.

Thursday 24th. Jan: 1889. At a meeting in the Round Room of the Tower Hotel this evening the following gentlemen formed themselves into a club.

Robert Anderson	John Turnbull
Findlay Purdon	Geo H. Wilson
Charles McL Purdon	John K. Purdon
Harold Evers	Willie Laing
Robert Blair	Robert Laing
James Blair	
Douglas Oliver	

It was resolved to call the Club the "Teviotdale Harriers" It's object to be the promotion of Athletics especially in the prosecution of Cross Country running during Winter months. The following office bearers were appointed for the season

John K. Purdon, Captain, Charles McPurdon
Geo. H. Wilson, Vice Do. Hon: Sec: & Treas:

It was decided to make a preliminary levy of 6d. per head to meet outlays.

The Captain was vested with full power to arrange runs, places of meet, paces, whips &c &c

It was arranged to meet at Brewery-yards on 26th inst. at 3.30, for a cross country run

Opening pages in the First Minute Book, recording the formation of the club.

On the 12th. of January 1889 the following 9 gentlemen met at Deanfield and had a preliminary run and at the close of the run it was resolved to call a meeting on the Thursday evening following of all who might be interested for the purpose of forming a Harriers Club:

John Turnbull,	Bank House	} Acting as Hares
Findlay Purdom,	Briery-yards	}
Geo. H. Wilson,	Deanfield	" " Whip
John R Purdom,	Briery-yards,	" " Pace
Douglas Oliver,	Thornwood	
Robert Blair,	Wilton Hill	
James Blair,	Do.	
Harold Evers,	Slitrig Crescent	
Robson,	Wilton Hill	

The Route chosen led from Deanfield by Wilton Dean, Whitehaugh hill, Lyonfield, Stouslee, Stouslee Cover, Galalaw, Stirches, Greenside hall & back. The day was fine and bright and the run was much enjoyed.

Distance about

JUBILEE DINNER

1889 1939

The Tower Hotel, Hawick
Friday, 20th January, 1939
At 7.30 p.m.

Chairman
Mr A. J. Grieve

Croupiers
Messrs J. M. Leydon and F. W. Innes

S. & P. HK.

The front cover, menu and toast list from the club's Jubilee Dinner programme, a report of which appears on pages 24 and 27. The toast to "The King" should have read Mr A. J. Grieve, Honorary President, the club president that season was Mr G. T. Harrower.

Menu

Soups.

Chicken Broth. Tomato.

Fish.

Fried Fillets of Sole.

Joints.

Beef Steak and Kidney Pie. Roast Beef.

Mutton and Ox Tongue (cold). Pickles.

Vegetables.

Potatoes and Mashed Turnips.

Sweets.

Fruit Salad. Plum Pudding.

Coffee.

Toast List

The King ... ... Mr A. J. Grieve, President.

Teviotdale Harriers' Club ... ... Mr G. L. McDonald.

Reply ... ... President.

Town and Trades of Hawick ... ... Mr T. Gillies.

Reply ... ... Provost Landles.

Kindred Clubs ... ... Mr T. H. Brydon.

Reply ... ... Mr G. M. Grant, E.N.H.

Our Guests ... ... Mr R. Crawford.

Reply ... ... Mr A. O. Robson, H.F.C.

Chairman and Croupiers ... ... Mr R. Christie.

Replies .. Mr J. M. Leyden & Mr F. W. Innes.

Accompanist ... ... *Mr Alex. Campbell.*

Harriers pictured outside the Old Stables in Wilton Park Road. The year is not known but it is possibly the oldest group photograph. Note the members with the shorts(?!) on the right of the group.

THE EARLY YEARS

ON SATURDAY, 12th JANUARY, 1889, nine Hawick men met at Deanfield on the outskirts of the town and took part in a cross-country run over some eight miles. The route chosen was via Wilton Dean, Whitehaughhill, Lyonfield, Stousalee, Stousalee Cover, Galalaw, Stirches, Greensidehall and back.

Those who took part were John R. Turnbull, Bank House and Findlay Purdom, Briery-yards, acting as "hares"; George H. Wilson, Deanfield, "whip"; John Purdom, Briery-yards, "pace"; Douglas Oliver, Thornwood; Robert Blair and James Blair, Wilton Hill; Harold Evers, Slitrig Crescent; and J. Robson, Wilton Hill. According to the first Minute Book, still in existence today, "the day was fine and bright and the run was much enjoyed."

At the conclusion of the run it was resolved to call a meeting of all who might be interested, "for the purpose of forming a Harriers club."

At this meeting, held in the Round Room of the Tower Hotel in Hawick on Thursday, 24th January, 12 gentlemen formed themselves into a club. Those already mentioned, with the exception of J. Robson, were joined by Robert Anderson, Charles McL. Purdom, Willie Laing and Robert Laing.

Again quoting from the first Minute Book: "It was resolved to call the club the Teviotdale Harriers. Its object to be the promotion of athletics especially in the prosecution of cross-country running during winter months."

The following office-bearers were appointed for the season:— John R. Purdom, captain; George H. Wilson, vice-captain; and Charles McL. Purdom, secretary and treasurer.

It was decided to make a preliminary levy of 6d (2½p) per head to meet outlays. The captain was vested with full power to arrange runs, places of meets, paces, whips, etc.

The first official run was arranged for Saturday, 26th January at 3.30 p.m. from Briery-yards and went via Littlecote, Teviotbank, Hassendean, Hassendeanburn, Home Farm and Midshiels, a distance of about eight miles. So began a club which, over the years, has overcome times when it was on the point of being disbanded, only to emerge even stronger until now, in this its centenary season, recognised as one of Scotland's leading clubs.

By the spring of 1889, membership had grown to 30 and their programme was a weekly run of some eight miles using the homes of members as a base. It was customary for the host to provide tea on their return, with the day ending with a smoker and entertainment. On occasion the Tennis Club Pavilion, St Cuthbert's Church School, Volunteer Park Pavilion, Hawick Football Club Pavilion and Hawick and Wilton Cricket Club Pavilion were used as starting off points.

In those early years two members were designated "hares"

A group of Harriers at the turn of the century, ready with their sacks of paper to lay the trail for the "hounds" to follow. Long shorts appear to be the height of fashion!

and it was their job to lay the trail using paper for their clubmates, the "hounds," to follow. The pack was led by a "pace" and a runner known as a "whip," bringing up the rear to attend to stragglers. Between 12 and 20 runners took part.

The first race to be arranged was a three-mile handicap with 13 members entering but no date for this was recorded in the Minute Book. In all probability it was some time in April 1889 to close the first season. The result was a win for topmarker W. Wight in 15 mins. 38 secs. from an allowance of 4 mins., followed by W. R. Porteous (allowed 3 mins.) 15 mins. 50 secs. Both men received a silver medal as their prize. Six members ran from scratch:— J. W. Glenny, G. H. Wilson, J. Turnbull, C. McL. Purdom, J. R. Purdom and J. Thomson.

At the close of the first season, in which 10 runs took place, the balance sheet showed a deficit of 2/3 (11p). Income came from 30 members' subscriptions at 6d (2½p), realising 15/- (75p) and 13 entries for the handicap at 3d (1p) realising 3/3 (16p). Expenditure amounted to 20/6 (£1.2½p) which included 18/6 (92½p) for two silver medals with engraving and 2/- (10p) for a notice board.

At the first general meeting held in the Tower Hotel on 5th October, 1889, it was arranged that the Buccleuch Hotel should be the club's headquarters.

It became common practice to arrange a "brake" to take members to Denholm five miles away and run back to Hawick.

Entries in the Minute Book which crop up quite regularly are calculations which make intriguing reading — though why so precise no one knows. The entry for the 1889-90 half-season states that the average attendance was 13-2/11ths members with 6-78/85ths minutes being the average time per mile! Highlights of 1890 were a "moonlight run" on a Wednesday evening leaving the Tennis Pavilion at 8.15, and the first inter-club run with Selkirk Harriers.

However, everything was not well for the club. At a committee meeting in February, 1890, it was stated that for some reason or other the number of members attending the runs seemed to be diminishing — at some only six turned out — and the question was, could nothing be done to increase the interest in the club. It was resolved on the motion of captain J. R. Purdom that for the future the pace was to be slower throughout and that there should be no racing at the end of the outing. But in December, because of a lack of interest in the club, there was no more runs in the 1890-91 season. In October, 1891, a meeting was held in the Tower Hotel at which it was decided to restart the club provided a sufficient number of members promised to turn out. It was agreed to issue membership cards with an annual subscription of 2/- (10p). The appeal for members appears to have been heeded as according to the "Hawick News" files, "a goodly number" began putting in an appearance for the weekly runs from Wilton Lodge Mansion.

This venue was to become a regular and indeed popular meeting place for the Harriers over the years. By the end of November the popularity of cross-country running was such that members were not satisfied with only one run a week and so Tuesday evening outings were started from the Exchange Hall.

Talking point of 1892 was undoubtedly a club run held in October which prompted mention in the columns of the "Hawick News." "While crossing a field at the back of St Leonards, four Highland cattle were observed grazing but on seeing the Maroons on their ground they made a gallant charge. The 'hounds,' thinking there would be one too many for them, showed the white feather by quickening the pace to a sprint, reaching the fence in a very exhausted condition. Some of them just cleared it in time to be saved a journey in the air."

It is in this extract from the local Press that the club colours are first mentioned and to this day no one knows why Teviotdale selected maroon. And even stranger is the fact that Gala Harriers chose green — a complete reversal of the rugby colours.

Also in 1892, in April, was held the now annual three-mile handicap and for the first time the venue was Hawick Moor — a course which was to feature in Harriers races to this day.

By now the club was in a much stronger position with regular runs on Saturdays, anything up to 14 miles; as well as on various week nights; a Tuesday afternoon section was formed with their own captain; a five-mile handicap was added in January, 1893; and monthly handicaps were arranged from November that year.

FIRST TROPHY

Surprisingly enough a club championship was not the first race for which a trophy was presented. At the annual general meeting in 1893 R. Bowie proposed a cup for the three-mile race, this being presented by patrons of the club and known simply as Teviotdale Harriers Cup. The magnificent 36-inch-high trophy was designed and supplied by F. E. Rutherford, jeweller. For the event 12 rules were drawn up, the most interesting being:—

No. 2—Cup to be won thrice before becoming the property of the winner.

No. 5—Every person must before being allowed to compete have taken part in at least six runs during that season.

No. 6—Entry money for the handicap shall always be 1/- (5p).

No. 12—Should the club become defunct the committee shall sell the Cup and remit the proceeds to the Cottage Hospital.

On facing page: A group of Harriers pictured in Wilton Lodge Park in the early 1900s. The trophy on top of the sacks of paper used to lay a trail is the Senior Cup. To date only A. J. Grieve (standing extreme left) and Junor Robertson (third from right in front row of six) have been recognised.

The inaugural race was to have been held on 31st March but this was postponed until 7th April when it was discovered that this would clash with the Gala v. Hawick rugby match!

In the three-mile race, four times round the racecourse, 13 started but only five managed to finish. The result was:—1, James Ferguson (allowed 3½ minutes) 18 mins. 45 secs.; 2, Frank Deans (3.00) 18.42; 3, Robert Campbell (2.30) 18.38.

In fourth place was Thomas Davidson who returned the fastest actual time of 16.59 and, according to the first Minute Book, "as far as could be remembered a record time for that distance."

The "Hawick News" described the race as "a very unexciting affair" and "uninteresting to a looker on."

A one-mile event after the Cup race for a medal presented by Mr F. Rutherford resulted as follows: — 1, Sam Nicholson (80 yards); 2, R. Russell (80 yards); 3, T. Davidson (scr).

To this day the Cup is held with such esteem that it is the ambition of all Harriers to win at the Moor, the championship taking second place.

The Cup race of 1895 was on a grand scale with valuable prizes. First was Robert Christie who received the Cup and a gold medal presented by Mr W. Edwards, surgeon dentist; second was James Ferguson who was awarded a marble clock presented by vice-president Dr Bannerman; third was Frank Deans who received a piece of tweed presented by Mr J. Graham Henderson, manufacturer, and fourth was John Pringle, who, having the fastest actual time, entitled him to a silver medal with a gold centre. The accompanying event on this occasion was a 100 yards handicap won by J. Elder who received a silver mounted biscuit barrel presented by club president Mr G. H. Wilson.

The thriving Harriers club was a source of great pleasure for members with 1894 ending with a run from Hawick Football Pavilion and an enjoyable game of football when they returned. New Year's Day 1895 was marked by an inter-club run, starting from the Victoria Hotel in the High Street, with Edinburgh Harriers, Edinburgh Northern Harriers, Newcastle Harriers and Berwick Harriers. This historic event was not only reported in the local Press but also in the "Glasgow Mail," "Scotsman" and "Evening News." In 1896 (1st January), 1898 (1st January) and 1899 (2nd January) both Edinburgh clubs and Teviotdale Harriers met at the Victoria Hotel prior to an outing in the country.

As has already been related, the local Press was a source for interesting accounts of club activities, such as the six-mile road-race introduced in March 1895, the route being "from the 51st to the 54th milestone on the Langholm road and back."

On facing page—
Runners from Teviotdale Harriers, Edinburgh Harriers and Edinburgh Northern Harriers, who met on New Year's Day 1896 for a cross-country run at Hawick. The photograph was taken at the rear of the now demolished Victoria Hotel in High Street and includes a porter, bellboy, waitress and barman.

The Tuesday section in 1912 or 1913, pictured in the grounds of Wilton Lodge Park with the Museum in the background.

But an even more amusing item headed "The Old Woman and the Harriers" under the "Rambler" column in the "Hawick News" of January 1896, must be quoted: "A good story is told of an old woman who had never heard of the Harriers. She had been walking 'up the Crescent' the other night when three redoubtables rushed past her. She came home and told her friends that she had got 'an aufu' fricht. Threi men cam past an' aw'm sure they must have broken oot o' the asylum, for they were half nakit an' rinnin' as if for their verra lives."

Yet another report tells of the time the Hawick club took the train to Melrose one Tuesday afternoon for a run in the area but the inhabitants of the town were "surprised and alarmed" at the sudden appearance of the Harriers.

The same thing happened in Selkirk. The Harriers drove to Drydenhope Farm where the farmer kindly granted leave to undress, their clothes being despatched to Selkirk by brake. The Souters were a "little alarmed" at the unexpected appearance of the large pack sprinting down their main street, reported the "Hawick News."

By 1894 the Harriers were well and truly established with 150 members and double that figure by the following year. It was in December 1895 that Teviotdale joined the Scottish Cross-Country Union and two years later the Scottish Border Amateur Athletic Association.

February 1896 saw the first mention of the club taking part in any open competition. This was the Scottish Junior Championship. The Hawick team got the fright of their lives when they turned up and saw the kind of men they were to run against. Though they had been training hard over the previous weeks the team did not finish with the required number to count.

The following month was the first scratch race promoted by the club, this being a 10-mile event won by Robert Christie in 61 mins. 15 secs.

The Cup race of that year was another milestone in the club's history, not that only six managed to finish from a field of 20 starters but that the club championship was henceforth to be decided from the fastest time returned at the Moor. The first title-holder, T. Davidson, received a gold medal, his time of 16 mins. 42.5 secs. being a record for the course. However, in 1906, the club championship was decided over a series of three races, with R. Grierson having a full number of points. Still on the history of the Cup race, records show that the event was switched from the race-course at the Moor to a cross-country course in 1898 but why remains a mystery. The route was from Wilton Lodge, round Borthaugh, Woodfoot and "Michie's" Bridge and down the "New Road" to the Toll House. The following year the race was due to have been run at Hawick Moor but because of a snowstorm it was cancelled and run on the following Monday night and the course — "2-2/5ths times round the cinder path at Wilton Lodge."

The Cup race in 1900 was also held in Wilton Lodge Park, on this occasion a Tuesday night.

Like other clubs, the Harriers had their social functions over the years, among them a Burns Supper, and an annual ball which in 1896 was described in the Press as "amongst the finest assemblies ever held in the town." Notable items in the club's history are many for the year 1896. A gate was adopted for club stationery in place of two runners as previously, the paper to have maroon lettering. The latter and the previously mentioned "Maroons" in a club run, are the only references to Teviotdale's colours which have come to light. At the annual general meeting in September 1896 they were faced with a membership problem. A motion raised that "members of Teviotdale Harriers must reside within a radius of six miles from Hawick." An amendment stated "any distance from Hawick." The motion was carried by 13 votes to 11. At a special general meeting two months later the same motion and amendment was among the business and once again the motion was passed this time by 11 votes to nine. However, the 1897 annual general meeting resolved to discontinue the rule that members must reside within six miles of Hawick. Also at this AGM was a move to change the club name to Hawick Harriers but this was defeated.

By now Teviotdale athletes were not content to rest during the summer months and several of them turned their attention to the track. The names who appear most are T. Davidson and R. Christie with a number of successes.

The century ended with Teviotdale Harriers enjoying a full programme of competition and social activities. Several new races had been introduced; there were monthly handicaps for the best attenders; inter-club runs with Jedburgh Harriers (and Gala Harriers in the near future); annual entry in the Scottish championships; and to crown it all, what a proud 1899 Common-Riding it was for Teviotdale with one of their members, Peter Robertson, chosen as Cornet.

During the seasons already mentioned several club runs were cancelled because it was raining — Harriers must have been less hardy then, unlike the present day when no matter what the weather, a club run or race goes ahead. In the last annual general meeting of the century, however, a motion was passed that in future "all ordinary club runs take place — wet or dry."

The 1898-99 season was brought to a close with an "At Home" in St James' Hall, believed to be the first function of its kind to be held in Hawick. Town Councillor Laidlaw received the guests on behalf of the club but his speech must have raised a few eyebrows among his hosts. He said he did not condemn athletics but he thought it was carried too far in Hawick to the detriment of the more elevating taste for literature. They should give more study to the wonderful history of Scotland and especially of their own Borderland. They ought to read the gems of poetry, literature and art which might be had in the Public Library. The "At Home" became an annual affair to bring a season to a close. Included at the function in 1900 was a presentation on behalf of the club of a handsome oak writing desk to the secretary, Thomas Davidson, in recognition of the work he had done in promoting the welfare of the club for the previous eight years. (Present day officials please note: do not plan in receiving similar gifts!).

Another Teviotdale social function was a Burns Supper. "The Harriers are the only athletic club in the town who kept a Burns nicht and had done so regularly for the past 10 years," so reported the "Hawick News" columns of 1902.

How many runners have heard of a "Toilet Handicap?" This novel event, staged at night, often concluded a season's activities. The competitors had to undress and put on running costume, run from Wilton Lodge to Martin's Bridge and down the "New Road" back to the Lodge where they dressed and finished the race. It can only be assumed that they undressed in the confines of the Lodge toilet—hence the name!

Another out-of-the-ordinary event was a walking race, the first of which was held in 1903. The race was a scratch one covering a 12-mile route from Wilton Lodge to "the seventh milestone up the Teviot and back." The winner was R. Wilson in 2 hrs. 5 mins 24 secs. The fastest time from one of the competitors was in the eighth mile in 10 mins. 1 sec. In all, Teviotdale now had eight official club races in the cross-country season ranging from one to eight miles.

JUNIOR SECTION FORMED

Such was the level of support the Hawick club was now receiving, in November 1907 it became necessary to form a junior section for which club officials procured a dressing room at Mrs Wilson's refreshment rooms at Wilton Lodge. They had an opening run of four miles in which nine young lads took part, the following week it was 40. Club officials were: — D. Houliston, captain; and R. Scott, secretary and treasurer. Their first race was in February the following year over a five-mile course, value 10/- (50p), 6/- (30p) and 4/- (20p), with D. Cavers winning from scratch in 35 mins. 58 secs. and in March 1909 the first junior 1½-mile event was held at the Moor on Cup race day. It was not until 1926 that a Junior Cup was introduced for competition at the Moor.

The highlight of the Harriers season in the early years was — and still is to this day — without doubt, the senior Cup race. By 1907 runners and spectators were conveyed to the Moor Racecourse by motor. Prior to this it was the custom to walk up to the Moor — a week night in those days — to undress and get into running costume outside, instead of from 1907, inside the race committee's rooms.

AMATEURISM v. PROFESSIONALISM

Time and again the virtues of amateurism were extolled at Harriers functions. At their "At Home" in 1907, members were advised to remain amateur as once a sport was taken up as a profession, it soon ceased to be a pleasure. In 1909 at their "At Home," Rev. Reid, rector of St Cuthbert's Episcopal Church presiding said: "In all athletics there were three dangerous tendencies — professionalism, betting and laziness. In a harriers club they had more chance to steer clear of these than in any other form of sport. If they were harriers they had to do the thing themselves, not to look on while others performed and as they aimed at pure, clean, sport, their club had a good deal to commend it to the community at large."

Over a 10-year period from 1904, seven names figured prominently in club activities, three of whom elevated to international fame.

FIRST INTERNATIONALIST

Adam J. Grieve, "Yid" as he was known, not only excelled on the track as a miler, winning the events at both Hawick and Melrose Sevens in 1905 and the Border championship on six occasions from 1905, to name but a few, he also wrote his name into the Harriers record books with some exceptional cross-country running. For several years he completely dominated Teviotdale races, for example in 1907, of the eight club events he won four of them. His performances in the Cup race were equally commendable, setting a new record in 1905 (16 mins. 34 secs.), 1907 (16.21) and 1908 (15.56). In 1907 he became the first Teviotdale Harrier to win the East of Scotland junior cross-country championship, the Hawick team finishing fourth that year. But his greatest achievement was a well merited selection for the Scottish team in the match against the Home Countries and

From 1896 to 1924 the club championships was decided from the fastest actual time in the 3-mile Senior Cup race, the winner receiving this gold medal.

Jimmy Grierson, a life-long supporter of the Harriers was the Eastern District Cross-Country Champion in 1913.

France in 1907. Unfortunately, according to the Press report, his leg "gave way" and he could only finish 43rd. Nevertheless, Grieve must have been very proud to be in such company with him coming from such a small, and at that time, young club.

ONLY OLYMPIC ATHLETE

"The best half-miler Scotland has yet produced, his strong finishes being a special feature of his running." This is how R. H. Burton, ranked as one of Teviotdale's greatest athletes, was described in the Press of 1909.

His father served his apprenticeship with Messrs A. Inglis, joiners, but the family moved to Tweedmouth. A member of both Teviotdale and Berwick Harriers, Burton had an especially warm side for the club of his native town.

The climax of his illustrious career on the track was his selection for the 1912 Olympic Games in Stockholm. However, writing home he said: "I turned out in my heat in the 800 metres but could not do what was asked of me." The occasion may have been too much for the humble Scot, who, up till then, had set the athletics track on fire with some outstanding performances. Six times between 1908 and 1912 he ran for Scotland in the half-mile, five of which were against Ireland, the other an Irish-American team; he won the Scottish half-mile championship in 1908, 1909 and 1910; added to this was the Border quarter-mile championship for four successive years from 1910; and broke the Scottish native half-mile record when finishing third in an invitation race at the Celtic Club's sports in 1910, knocking two-fifths of a second off the existing 1 min. 58-4/5ths secs. which had stood since 1905.

Hawick R.F.C. captain and Scottish internationalist W. R. Sutherland also made a name for himself on the running track. He was Border champion in both the 100 yards and 220 yards in 1911-12-13 and 14, with times such as 10.4 secs. and 23.2 secs. respectively. However, it was as a track internationalist that he will be best remembered. He ran against Ireland in 1911 and 1913, and England in 1913. In the 1913 international against Ireland, "Suddy" as he was known, won the 220 yards in 22.6 secs., a personal best and a time which had only twice been bettered in the history of the contest. The "Edinburgh Evening News" said: "Sutherland's running was the sensation of the match. The Hawick man ran the race of his life."

As well as setting a number of cross-country club records, one which had stood for 13 years, Jimmy Grierson was Eastern District champion in 1913. That year Teviotdale had the distinction of having the first two individuals to finish with Tommy Hamilton in second place. The Hawick team was fourth, the championship being won by none other than Gala Harriers!

Hamilton, James K. Burns and Robert Grierson were all prominent in club events at that time.

WYOMING CHALLENGE CUP

Between the years 1909-1913 a star attraction at the Common-Riding Games was a one-mile team relay for the Wyoming Silver Challenge Cup presented by Hawick Callants in Wyoming, U.S.A. Valued at 22 guineas, the solid silver cup weighing over 70 ounces, was supplied by F. E. Rutherford, jeweller, Hawick and was according to the rules, "open to all amateur harriers clubs in Great Britain and Ireland." Intimation of the handsome 18-inch high cup in the form of a loving cup with three handles, was sent by Teri "exile" Mr Frank Deans who had taken a great interest in athletic events when in Hawick. His initiative in procuring 20 subscribers was evidence of the interest he and the other "exiled" Teries had of their native town.

Custody of the cup developed into a real ding dong affair. West of Scotland were the winners in 1909, with Teviotdale third. The Hawick club won in 1910, the team being A. J. Grieve, W. R. Sutherland, J. S. Turnbull and R. H. Burton. It went back to the West the following year, with Teviotdale second, their team being the same as 1910 except for J. M. Ballantyne replacing Turnbull. The cup returned to Hawick in 1912, thanks to T. Bell, Ballantyne, Sutherland and Burton, with West runners-up. The situation for the 1913 race was such that each club had two wins to their credit and the rules stated that three wins would give absolute custody. That year it once again went to West of Scotland and so they claimed permanent possession. Teviotdale's team of Bell, A. Anderson, Sutherland and Burton, were runners-up.

Investigation since has revealed that the West team (J. H. Rodger, R. C. Duncan, H. J. Christie and G. Dallas) contrary to the rules laid down for the competition, did not comprise a full complement of first-claim members, the last named being from Maryhill Harriers, and so in actual fact should have lost the cup by default.

The cup was put up for competition by the West of Scotland in their area, was won outright by another club and is now in the hands of the Scottish Amateur Athletic Association and presently for the national 4 x 100 metres relay championship.

The Common-Riding Games of 1914 included a team relay race but no trophy. Again the West of Scotland won, with Teviotdale's team of Bell, Sutherland, Ballantyne and Grieve, runners-up. The event was not run again until 1920.

Returning to December 1900, Teviotdale Harriers entertained two of their members to a supper in Pringle's Temperance Hotel when they were presented with gold medals on the occasion of their return from active service in South Africa. Dr Bannerman, president, in welcoming the pair on behalf of the club, said that it was improbable that they would have to welcome back members from another war. How wrong he was to be.

The Teviotdale team who won the Wyoming Cup in the medley relay at Hawick Common-Riding Games in 1910. They are (standing, left to right)—W. R. Sutherland and A. J. Grieve, and (seated) J. S. Turnbull and R. H. Burton.

At the annual general meeting on 8th September, 1914, it was decided that owing to the present crisis (World War I) office-bearers should remain "en bloc" and subscriptions to be voluntary. There would be no races but weekly runs would be continued when possible and members to pay a levy of 1d or 2d each run. That day alone 30 Harriers from the membership of 140 responded to the call to Lord Kitchener's forces. No activities were recorded in the club's Minute Book or the local Press until the war was over.

In March 1915, at the S.B.A.A.A. annual general meeting it was stated that there was very little prospect of any athletic meetings being held during the summer as between five and six hundred members of the affiliated clubs had joined the Colours, representing 85% of the active members and 50% of the total membership.

MAKING A NEW START

The annual general meeting in September, 1919, marked the restart of the club but among members killed in action were club secretary A. Anderson and internationalist W. R. Sutherland.

Saturday and Tuesday runs were started straight away, the old headquarters at the Douglas Temperance Hotel was secured again and the Swimming Baths and the room at Wilton Lodge were used as starting off points. Teviotdale Harriers were back in full swing. The first official race, a six-mile handicap was run in the November with D. McMinn the winner. By 1920 the membership was 130. The first Cup race since 1914 was run in March 1920 with twice winner W. Boyd competing adding greatly to the interest. The majority of the field were first-year lads. James Armstrong won the Cup and with R. Smith recording the fastest time, was presented with the club championship medal.

Throughout the 1920s, Teviotdale were favoured with strong support, the membership ranging from 125 to just over 200 by the end of the decade.

In 1923, the club began their evening sports meetings in the Volunteer Park which were to become a regular feature over the years. On the non-competitive side of activities, there were regular inter-club runs with Gala Harriers and Selkirk Harriers and there was even an annual inter-section rugby match when the Saturday and Tuesday sections of the club changed their sport for the day.

In 1925 the club championship changed from being the fastest time in the Cup race at the Moor to a seven-mile race, with a sealed handicap in January.

ANOTHER SCOTTISH CHAMPION

Four names figured in athletics during the decade. Teviotdale had another Scottish champion and internationalist in their ranks when Ian Sutherland won the 1927 national 100 yards title in 10.6 seconds and from this performance was chosen to run for his country in the 100 yards in a triangular international finishing third, followed by selection for the 100 yards and 220 yards for the match against Achilles (Oxford and Cambridge "blues"), finishing second in each.

At club level, as well as Sutherland in the sprints, Teviotdale had G. T. Harrower as a prominent miler, while over the country, 1921 club champion A. McPhail was runner-up in the Eastern District Championship that year. And, of course, there was D. L. Erskine. Five times Teviotdale cross-country champion successively from 1922, such was his domination of club events that in an eight-mile handicap, for example, he conceeded starts of up to eight minutes and in the 1923-24 season alone collected five prizes.

ERIC LIDDELL AT HAWICK

The Amateur Games at Hawick Common-Riding in the 1920s was held on alternate Fridays and Saturdays yearly, with the attraction in 1922-23-24 being the appearance of that Scottish "great," Eric Liddell. Several Hawick runners competed against him in the sprints with some measure of success but of course, from big starts, Liddell being off scratch.

In the 1922 100 yards, Teviotdale's D. Gordon, off 9 yards, knocked out Liddell in the heats and went on to be runner-up in the final. At that time the first prize was 120/- (£6) value — quite an amount in those days. That day Gordon won the 220 yards handicap, value 80/- (£4) off 20 yards.

Scottish sprint champion Liddell was back again in 1923 and on this occasion won both the 100 yards (10.4 secs.) and 220 yards (23.2 secs.), with Gordon, off 17 yards, runner-up in the furlong event. The one-mile team race that year was won by Edinburgh University; their team including Liddell. Teviotdale was third.

In 1924, the year of his Olympic Games triumph, Eric ran in the Common-Riding sprint at the Volunteer Park, figuring in a controversial finish to the 100 yards. The Press described the final as "a rare scamper." One judge gave the verdict to Bill Turnbull, Teviotdale, off 8 yards, but two gave clubmate Hector Innes (10 yards) first, with Liddell (scr.) second and Athey of Edinburgh third. The last named asked the judges if they were blind or just "blind drunk" as he had pulled up and watched the finish from the rear. Liddell was confident that there were two in front of him. The incident caused a row in athletic circles and neither Liddell nor Athey would accept their prizes. The "Hawick News" file for that week gives the result as: 1, Hector Innes; 2, Eric Liddell; 3, Bill Turnbull. The one unanimous verdict in the controversial issue, however, was that Liddell was a sportsman and a gentleman. Turnbull had the satisfaction and the honour of beating Liddell in the sports at Galashiels two months later when, off 6 yards, he pipped him in the heat.

Liddell returned to the Borders in the November of that year for an evangelist meeting at Galashiels but prior to this he spoke to members of Gala Harriers saying: "One can usually manage to get through a game of rugby when only half fit but no one can go on to a cinder track and win a race without being perfectly fit. It is during the period of training that the best qualities of a man are developed and it is showing sufficient grit to go on and bringing out that spirit of determination to go through which made the successful athlete. Athletics brought out that spirit of determination to get to the top in whatever sphere of sport they went into and it was only when that spirit was attained that they could hope for success."

The moving story of Eric Liddell, from Olympic champion to a missionery in China and his subsequent death in a Japanese prison camp, was told world-wide with the making of the award-winning film "Chariots of Fire." In the Borders it stirred up memories for Hector Innes, resident in Kelso, and Bill Turnbull of Hawick.

COMMON-RIDING "MARATHON"

At this period, the 1920s, Hawick Common-Riding Games included a "marathon." This was how it was described in the results of the Games in the columns of the "Hawick News" but measurements in those days must have been different from those now — the race was only 5½ miles! The course was to Michie's Bridge and back then 2½ times round the Volunteer Park track. In the 1922 race, the winner was Teviotdale's J. Cooper (allowed 3 mins 30 secs.) in 28 mins. 1.6 secs. Cooper, who won by about a circuit of the track from the Gala Harriers club captain H. Flannigan, was carried off the field in triumph by a number of his fellow Harriers.

At Hawick in 1927, the Scottish Border Amateur Athletic Association inaugurated the first championship meeting, instead of farming out individual championships among the various clubs and organisations in the Borders.

Included among Teviotdale's cross-country activities was participation in the Eastern District Championship, which in 1929, was staged in Hawick. On that occasion the Hawick club finished sixth, R. E. E. Stewart being the best placed finishing 12th. Runners-up in the team competition were Gala Harriers, at that time a much stronger club than Teviotdale.

On facing page: Teviotdale's team in the 1929 Eastern District Championships. Back row (left to right)—John Campbell, Fergus Hunter, Leslie Fitzwalter, George Stenhouse, Robert Stewart, James Patterson. Front row—Andrew Kyle, James Jamieson, Frank Elliot, James Telfer, Thomas Jamieson, James Marchbank.

Opening run of the 1921-22 season. The captain is Bob Crawford (seated centre with dark sash).

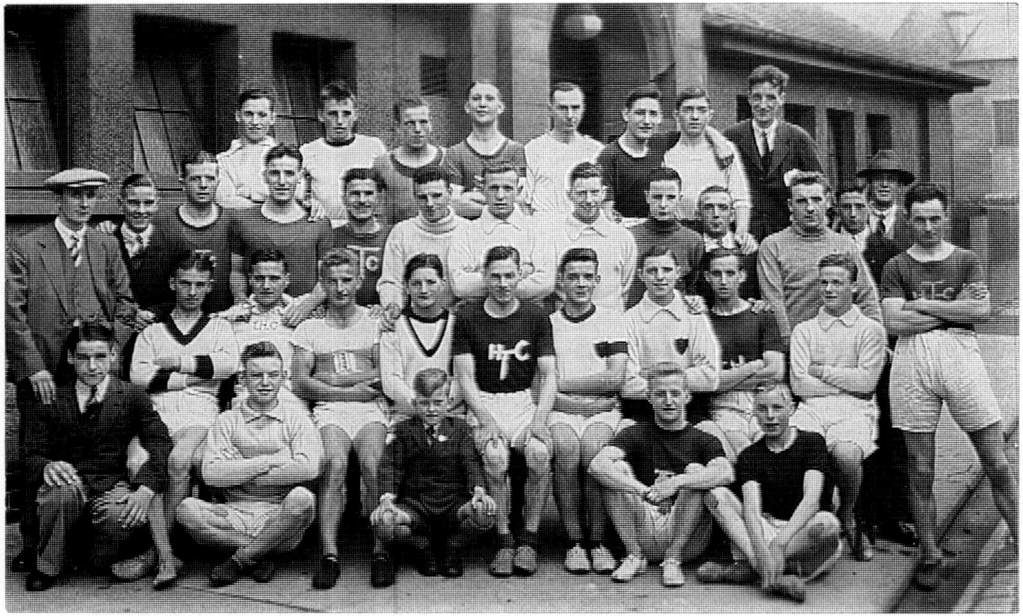

Opening run of the 1930-31 season.

LADIES' SECTION FORMED

The main item of activity in 1930 was the formation of a ladies' section. A special meeting was held in St James' Hall on 8th September to which ladies interested in cross-country running and athletics were invited. Thirty enthusiastic ladies turned up and elected the following office-bearers:— captain—Betty White; vice-captain—Isa Maguire; secretary—Chrissie Hood; committee—Ada White, Rita Willieson and Mary Murray.

Mr R. Crawford, club treasurer, presiding, told those attending that in the event of them forming a club he would advise them not to overdo it in the first year. They would fall into the routine of cross-country runs very easily and it would be an exhilarating way of spending their Saturday afternoon. He did not think there was any harm in girls wearing the regulation shorts. A subscription of 2/6 (12½p) was fixed and an opening run planned for Saturday, 4th October. For that first run 36 ladies "stripped" at the Baths. The event caused considerable interest in the town there being several hundred spectators anxious to see the new venture. J. M. Richardson, J. E. Duff and W. J. Walker of the male section accompanied as instructors over a three-mile course via Overhall, Whitehaugh, Scawmill, Wilton Dean and home by Blaikie's Brae.

The first race for ladies was held on December 20th over a 1½-mile course. The event started at a point on the high road in Wilton Lodge Park near to the Waterfall and the course was by Wood's Nurseries, the Dunk, across Langlands Bridge and down the New Road, finishing in the Upper Haugh. The result was:— 1, E. Mitchell (allowed 60 secs) actual time 12 mins. 15 secs.; 2, L. Harrower (.20) 11.55; 3, R. Horne (scr.) 11.39. They competed for their first championship at the Moor on the 1931 Cup race day over a ¾-mile course which was won by Ruby Horne.

Coming back to the male section, two trophies were presented to the club in 1932, one for a cross-country event and the other the first for a track race. The latter, for the 100 yards championship, was the Scott Trophy, presented by Mr John H. Scott, a former Teviotdale official. J. R. Purdom, the Club's first captain and invested as a life member in 1931, presented the Langheugh Trophy in 1932, to be run over a 6-mile course. Langheugh was the name of his house in Buccleuch Road.

On the social side, the 1935 dinner had Dr Simpson proposing the toast to the club. He told the assembled company: "Teviotdale has tasted the fruits of victory against near neighbours and against competitors further afield and it had also had its bitterness of defeat but it was only those victories and alternate defeats that made the game worth while."

Presiding at the gathering was John Purdom. He told his fellow Harriers that the club was first formed with the idea of providing clean, honest, healthy sport and was sure that all men

The first ladies' section opening run on 4th October, 1930, pictured outside the Public Baths. Included in the group are Betty White (captain), Margaret Edgar, Mary Hogg, Peggy Dalgleish, Lizzie Harrower, Isa McGuire, Maimie McLaughlan, Ada Wight, Chrissie Hook, Janet Beattie, Patricia Tierney, Phoeme Mitchell, Rita Willison, Ruby Horne, Isa Cummings, Amy Johnstone and Nessie Fiddes (trainer).

of the club who had been taking advantage of the privileges of the club would bear him out when he said that the club had justified its existence and had carried out the spirit in which it was born. He was certain it would continue to do so.

By the 1936-37 season, however, the club was mourning the death of Mr Purdom and for the entire year black-draped vests were worn as a mark of respect.

SCOTTISH CHAMPIONSHIPS

In the Scottish championships of 1932 W. Hogg was second in the pole vault with a height of 10′ 6″. He was decidedly unlucky in that he got well over 11′ to tie the title when a gust of wind blew his pole back against the bar, knocking it down. However, consolation came Hawick's way in 1936 when George Stanger won the youths' 100 yards championship. In his heat he ousted the holder, returning the fastest time of the day, 10.1 secs. and in the final 10.4. Though not a member of Teviotdale at the time, he joined shortly after and was to figure in club contests and the club championship.

Prominent Harriers of the 1930-39 period included T. H. Jamieson, P. McDonald, A. Valentine, R. E. Scott, I. Curruthers, brothers B. Smith and W. B. Smith and last but by no means least, P. Armstrong. Phil was a noted miler, enjoying complete dominance over the distance, as well as being a successful cross-country runner. He was eighth in the Eastern District Cross-Country Championship in 1937. It was once said of him "he was like the proverbial brook — he went on and on forever."

50th ANNIVERSARY

Four things dominated the 1938-39 season — January 1939 the club's jubilee was celebrated; they gained their first ever Scottish cross-country team championship in March; two trophy races were introduced; but then later in the year war was declared.

The club's jubilee was celebrated by a dinner in the Tower Hotel with guests from sporting clubs in the Borders and other parts of Scotland, there was even the Spanish Vice-Consul from Edinburgh, Senor José Lopez Roura, who came as a guest of William Jardine, Edinburgh, a member of Teviotdale 46 years previous.

The toast "Teviotdale Harriers Club" was proposed by G. L. McDonald, life member and former official. Honorary president A. J. Grieve replying said that they were banded together for the love of their sport and for the pleasure they derived from it and not for

Harriers line up for the start of the first Langheugh Trophy race in 1932. Included is Mr J. R. Purdom who donated the new trophy. He was the club's first captain in 1889 and the race got its name from his house in Buccleuch Road. The competitors are (left to right)—T. H. Jamieson, G. E. Stenhouse, J. M. Richardson, G. Oliver, A. Fox, T. H. Brydon, J. M. Leyden (winner), F. Innes, W. Newbigging, J. Laidlaw, A. Laidlaw and W. B. Gray.

The 220 yards invitation event at the S.B.A.A.A. championship meeting in the Volunteer Park, Hawick, in 1933. They are (left to right)—Dr F. P. Reid, Atalanta (scr.); A. Kennedy, Gala Harriers (9 yds.); I. Sutherland, Teviotdale (9 yards); and R. E. Scott, Teviotdale (14 yards), the winner.

any mercenary reason. He had seen them win their races but he had also seen them, like good sportsmen, accept defeat when fortune, in its fickle mood, had declared against them. And, after all, that was the real spirit of all sport. He would ask them to compare the looker on with the young fellows who returned from their sport with the blood coursing faster through their veins and the joy of living in their hearts, for the man or youth who had never been fit had never lived.

To celebrate jubilee year a trophy was presented by Mr G. L. McDonald to be competed for over a $3\frac{1}{2}$-mile course and to be known appropriately enough as the Jubilee Trophy. The first race was held on 28th January with Bert Smith the winner, while he and his older brother W. Smith shared the fastest actual time of 23 mins. 50 secs.

Also to commemorate Teviotdale's jubilee year, the Eastern District Championships were staged in Hawick and it must have given the host runners an added boost. That day they finished runners-up with 104 points to Edinburgh University, 85 points, followed by Dundee Hawkhill, 134. The Teviotdale team was: 4, W. Smith; 7, B. Smith; 16, P. Armstrong; 17, G. Easton; 29, D. Spalding; 31, W. Knox.

TEVIOTDALE'S FIRST SCOTTISH CROSS-COUNTRY TEAM CHAMPIONSHIP

In March, Teviotdale were the only East of Scotland team to enter for the Scottish cross-country youths' championship. Against 22 clubs from the West of Scotland, the Hawick callants finished 25 points ahead of nearest rivals Motherwell, with the following team counters:—3, G. Easton; 7, B. Smith; 8, D. Spalding; 23, W. Boyd. Those "in the know" in Harriers circles locally, however, were not unduly surprised at the team's success. It had been recognised that not for many years had they possessed so many promising young runners.

Before emigrating to Australia, Jim Menzies, who had been treasurer for a number of years and club captain in the 1925-26 season, presented a cup in his name. The Menzies Trophy race was designated a five-mile event with J. Scott the first holder.

In September 1939, once again a world war was declared and once again members were quick to join the Colours. At the annual general meeting in October it was decided that the club should go on with the season's runs, except that there would be no races and no trophies would be competed for.

For the next six years, the club's Minute Book does not record any activities, though Press reports in January 1940 stated that Teviotdale sent a team to take part in an inter-club run at Galashiels with Gala Harriers and Edinburgh University, and in March in an inter-club run between Teviotdale and Gala Harriers at Hawick, soldiers were included in both teams.

Opening run of the 1932-33 season.

Opening run of the 1936-37 season.

The 1936-37 Tuesday section opening run. The sub-captain is W. Nichol (seated, third left).

Teviotdale's first Scottish Cross-Country Team Championship. The juniors who ran at Lanark in March 1939 are (back row, left to right)—G. Harrower (trainer), D. Spalding (8th), J. Boyd (23rd) and W. Cuthbertson, and (front row)—B. Smith (7th), G. Easton (3rd) and E. Murray. The team had 41 points to Motherwell's 67.

MAKING A START ONCE MORE

At a meeting in the Library Hall in March 1946, to revive the club once the war was over, members were upstanding for a minute's silence in token of their respect for those fellow Harriers — Phil Armstrong, Tom Young, Bert Turnbull, Robert Richardson, Jack Smith and Peter Kerr — who had made the supreme sacrifice. It was decided to form a temporary committee to carry on the club meanwhile until the A.G.M. in September. Many of the pre-war members indicated their willingness to turn out the next season to encourage young members.

At the September meeting it was intimated that as club funds amounted to only £30 it would be difficult to provide prizes so it was suggested that dances be arranged to raise money. The fees were to remain as before at 3/- (15p) seniors, 2/- (10p) juniors. The opening runs on 5th October, 1946 (Saturday section) and 8th October (Tuesday section) marked the restart after a lapse of six years, followed by an inter-club run in November with Gala Harriers and the first race, the Menzies Trophy, won by J. Douglas. So once again the Harriers were able to pick up the pieces and reshape their club.

Mr G. L. McDonald, donor of the Jubilee Trophy started the 1947 race won by Willie Knox off scratch but in that same month, February, the heavy snow of that winter not only resulted in the Langheugh Trophy race being postponed but cancelled all together — the first and only time this has happened. The following month the Cup race at the Moor racecourse was postponed owing to deep snow but it was rescheduled for the evening of Tuesday, 1st April and run over a 3-mile course in Wilton Lodge Park. The start was at the Bowling Green then twice round the Park from the Laurie Bridge to the top end of the Dunk. It was last run in the Park 47 years previously after it was postponed for a similar reason.

Talking point of the Cup race in 1948 was the remarkable achievement of J. M. Leyden in winning at the age of 43. "Pimmy" as he was known, was, it will be recalled, the first winner of the Langheugh Trophy in 1932. He was quite a character, what one would call a "worthy." At the 1948 dinner he remarked that it had taken him 26 years to win the Cup!

Proposing the toast to the club at that function, that Harriers' stalwart Bob Crawford summed up the comradeship that had now built up in Teviotdale saying: "A club which could maintain existence for such a period had proved that it fulfilled a want and had justified its existence." To non-prizewinners he said: "You should never lose heart as racing was not the primary function of the club but rather healthy recreation after a week's work. At the same time it did give the club a boost when honours came to it."

On facing page: The opening run of the 1939-40 season. They are (back row, left to right)—G. P. Turnbull, R. E. Scott, W. Knox, H. Nivet, W. B. Gray, J. Leyden (captain), J. Liddle, R. Leithead (vice-captain), J. Boyd, A. Richardson, J. A. C. Murray, G. Lumsden, J. Campbell, G. Yeoman, R. Crawford. Front row—J. Marshall, C. Morrison, S. Reid, G. Reid, J. Foster, G. Scott, J. McHugh and T. H. Jamieson.

Space does not permit the inclusion of all club activities in this 100-year history but some items just cannot go unmentioned. In 1949, at a meeting of the Teviotdale ladies' section a basketball team was formed. The same year, James Menzies, the club member who had emigrated to Australia in 1939, sent food parcels to be used as prizes, food rationing being still in operation in Britain. The famous Trinidadian sprinter E. Macdonald Bailey won the 100 yards in 9.8 secs. at the 1951 Hawick Common-Riding Games and the amateur star accepted an invitation to compete at a Harriers evening sports meeting the following month before a crowd estimated at 5000. George P. Turnbull, winner of the senior Cup race in 1939 and 1949, won it outright in 1951. The only other double winners up to that year were R. Christie (1895 and 1897) and W. Boyd (1909 and 1914) but it was the "veteran" 38-year-old George who was first to make it a "hat-trick." Sportingly and thankfully he made the fine gesture of handing the Cup back for future competition with the proviso that if the club should ever be wound up the Cup should go to his family. In 1955 W. "Barty" Yule won the Cup to be followed by wins in 1968, 1970 and 1973 — a feat unequalled to this day.

THE 1950s REVIEWED

The Harriers in the late 1940s and early 1950s could be termed as more of a social club than an athletics club, especially during the cross-country season.

Club runs followed the same pattern as they had done for many years. Members reported at the Swimming Baths at 2 p.m. on Saturdays every week without fail whether it was good weather or deep snow and no run was ever cancelled because of the weather. The members were split into two packs — fast pack and slow pack — and the captain appointed a pace and whip for each pack. A Tuesday pack was still in existance for members who worked in shops but fell away as more people started working in the hosiery factories. On several occasions the club run was to Jedburgh but in each case only a handful managed to last the course over the Dunion.

Though there were about five races during the season for club trophies, there was not much in the way of competitive spirit and for most the main reason for being members of the Harriers was just as a means of exercise and keeping fit. As an added interest, inter-club runs were held with Gala Harriers and Edinburgh Southern Harriers and many friendships were formed as a result.

The highlight of the cross-country season was to run in the Eastern District Championship which was the only race the club entered for at that time.

Training consisted of meeting at the Baths on Wednesday nights for a run round Martin's Bridge. This was as far as they could run — not because of the lack of ability — but by the time they got back and had a shower it was time for the Baths to close.

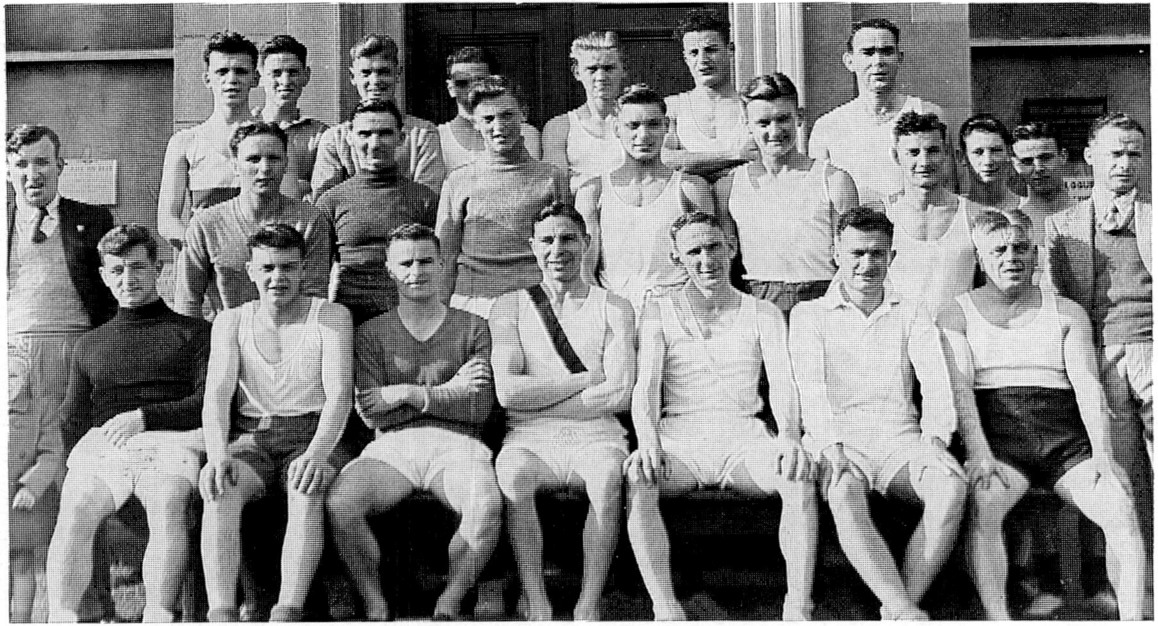

A group of Harriers in the 1950s pictured outside Hawick Museum.

Any other form of training was done on their own from their own home — not a very good arrangement — so it became obvious that clubrooms were needed.

When one considers what took place in the way of training there were several good cross-country runners in the club in the 1950s and, had there been more competition in the area, athletes such as Jack Hogg, Jim Elliot, Ken Borthwick, Douglas Campbell, Dick Wilkinson and "Paddy" Lawrence would have made a good team in any open event. But more about some of these runners later.

Unlike today, it did not require much money to run the club in the 1950s. In the cross-country season, winners would receive a trophy and voucher for 30/- (£1.50), runners-up would get £1 and third 15/- (75p) and the vouchers could be traded in at several local shops. There would also be races for juniors but there were not many runners and consisted mainly of 15 to 17-year-olds.

During this time Teviotdale branched out into other sports. They had a team which regularly participated in the Hawick Basketball League and had a team in the Royal Albert six-a-side football tournament.

For many years the traditional start to the cross-country season was the Sunday after the opening run in September when club members walked to Cavers Church for the morning service.

The highlight to end the cross-country season was — and still is — the annual dinner which, in the 1950s was held in the Victoria Hotel. It was always an enjoyable evening, so much so that the same guests looked forward to being there year after year. John Gavin, Gala Harriers, was always a regular, as was Jimmy Mitchell, Edinburgh A.C. A number of well known personalities were invited as main speakers, including Olympic athlete Jim Alder and "Ming" Campbell and another, well known in Scottish coaching circles, was Alex. Naylor from Glasgow. Everyone had to give a turn and it is said that some of the worst singers ever heard gave their vocal chords an airing at the Harriers dinner but once the trophies had been duly filled and passed round, everyone agreed the singers "improved!" The exceptions, of course, were the official guest entertainers. Bert Armstrong, whose fine voice was much enjoyed and the ever popular Willie Lightheart at the piano, were both regular attenders for many years and great supporters of the Harriers.

Track runners in the 1950s had more competition than the cross-country section, with several meetings taking place in the area. Peebles, Jedburgh, Berwick and Duns had amateur clubs and regularly held their own sports meetings. Teviotdale and Gala Harriers, the main clubs, each ran two or three meetings during

Captain J. Elliot (centre, with dark sash) leads the pack on the opening run of the 1952-53 season.

the season. These events, as well as inter-club contests, meant that athletes had quite a busy season.

Several local rugby players took part in these summer meetings, especially in the sprints and included Bert Hume, Jack Blaikie, Bill Wallace and Duncan Gordon, who figured in the prize lists on many occasions. The majority of cross-country athletes also took part on the track, mainly in the middle distance events, and no mile event was complete without such names as Jack Hogg, Jim Elliot, Ken Borthwick, George Wright, W. Armstrong, Douglas Campbell, Jock Carruthers, Benny Murray and Dick Wilkinson, to name but a few, with a young W. "Barty" Yule and Grant Moyes starting off their long association with the club.

The mid 1950s brought a new crop of athletes to the track scene with regular — and some highly successful — competitors in the sprints, such as Wullie Gray, Vic Law, Ian Bell, Jake Coltman, George Gibb, Harry Murphy, Jim Glendinning, Charlie March and Ronnie Pringle. In the distance events some well known names began to appear, such as Rob Crozier, who had been reinstated from the professional ranks, Bruce Glendinning, Billy Riddell, John Hamilton and two young runners who were to figure prominently for the next few years, Jim Jack and Keith Harley.

But track athletes in the Borders were to have a few lean years ahead. The Peebles and Jedburgh clubs folded, Gala Harriers were left with only a few members and Teviotdale was to lose a number to the professional circuit in the coming years as the amateur meetings disappeared.

WELL KNOWN AMBASSADORS

Three individuals, who, though never reaching international level, became among Teviotdale's most well known ambassadors.

Douglas Campbell won the junior championship in 1949-50-51. Not anything unusual one might say but the 16-year-old also won the senior championship the same three years — the first time such a "double" had been achieved and a feat never repeated since. He even went one better in also winning the Tuesday section championship in 1949. In winning the 1951 senior championship, Douglas became the first holder of the Campbell Trophy which had been donated to the club by his father, John, a prominent Harrier in the 1930s who later devoted much of his time to officiating. Space does not allow full coverage of Douglas Campbell's phenomenal run of track successes. He was a frequent competitor in the mile handicap which used to be run between the semi-final and final at the rugby sevens tournaments at Hawick and Melrose. In 1955 Douglas clipped 3.2 secs. off G. T. Harrower's club record for that distance which had stood since 1926.

Opening run of the 1953-54 season. Club captain is Dick Wilkinson (seated in centre with dark sash).

THE "LOCAL ZATOPECK"

H. "Paddy" Lawrence, the first Teviotdale Harrier to indulge in extensive training, was rewarded for his efforts with a domination never before encountered in the Hawick club. In 1954, in winning the 12-mile Carluke road-race the Press reported "the field found 'Paddy's' pace too hot," in fact that year he won every road-race he entered — Helenvale 15-mile, Renfrew 15-mile and the Aberfeldy 14-mile in which he beat British marathon champion Joe McGhee's road-race record by over half a minute. He could hold his own with some of the top names in Scottish distance running. In the Scottish six-mile track championship, "Paddy" finished runner-up to record-holder Ian Binnie of Victoria Park. The "local Zatopeck" as he was nicknamed by the Press, won only one handicap trophy in his illustrious career but re-wrote the record books with his amazing turn of speed. Four times in succession from 1953 he won the seven-mile senior cross-country championship, setting a new record in three of them — in 1953 he clocked 39 mins. 35 secs, the following year it was 38.42 and in 1955 he brought it down to 38.37. In 1952 he smashed the Menzies Trophy record by 1 min. 7 secs, the following year the Menzies and Langheugh Trophy records tumbled by 40 secs. and 19 secs. respectively and in 1956 he clipped a further 10 secs. off the Jubilee Trophy record.

No sooner had Campbell and Lawrence found their running days were over than another began to carve a name for himself both on the track and over the cross-country — this was Jim Jack. He first came into the limelight in 1953 when he finished second in the Eastern District junior championship. In 1957 he reduced Campbell's mile record by 1.6 secs. and then two years later shattered his own record for the event by 5.6 secs. His success on the track would fill several pages. Over the cross-country, records tumbled as well. In 1958 Jim broke Lawrence's 1953 Cup race record by 10 secs., bringing the three-mile time down to 18 mins. 21 secs.; then in 1959 a further three of Lawrence's records fell to him. The Jubilee Trophy record went by 59 secs., the Menzies by 25 secs. and the club championship record by six secs., reducing the 7-mile time to 38 mins. 31 secs. In 1960 Jim smashed his Cup race record by 26 secs. In Jim Jack's shadow at this time was Rob Renton, Border mile champion for three successive years from 1958 who, along with Jim, made club history by recording the only dead-heat in the 7-mile club championship, this was 1958.

The cross-country junior club championship had been an official race since 1925 but it was not until 1956 that the title holder received a trophy. The new award was presented by Benny Murray and named in his honour. The donor was the winner of the Menzies Trophy in 1949 and 1950, one of only two Harriers to retain this cup; the other was Arthur Oliver (1966-67).

Captain H. "Paddy" Lawrence (seated fourth left) with those who turned out in the 1954-55 opening run.

Opening run of the 1955-56 season.

The 1956-57 opening run.

The opening run of the 1957-58 season with club captain Maxwell Shankie (back row, second right, with the dark sash).

Cross-country and track club champion Jim Jack. This is Jim breasting the tape to win the Border 3-mile title in 1958.

George Wright winning the 880 yards title in the 1958 Border Championships.

Keith Harley, pictured after retaining the Junior Cup in 1958.

Rob Wharton, winner of the Senior Cup race in 1958.

BUILDING CLUBROOMS

A milestone in the club's history was building clubrooms but it was a long drawn out affair and a hard struggle, before their dreams came true.

As has already been said, in the early years the Harriers used various venues as headquarters, then around the turn of the century and for some 20 years, they rented two rooms behind the Mansion House, now the Museum, in Wilton Lodge Park. A feature of the runs from there was the tea and scones supplied by Mrs Whitelaw, wife of the park-keeper. It was common in the early days for the runners to spend two or three hours after the runs enjoying an impromptu concert as there was no movies in Hawick at the time, consequently there was no rush to get away for the "first house." The washing facilities were those of Mrs Whitelaw's washhouse. Many a mud-stained Harrier had a pail of water sloshed over him.

The Public Swimming Baths were used as stripping quarters for the next 25 years but when frost-bound sports pitches caused cancellations, the Baths were closed and the Harriers forced to improvise. This state of affairs led to depleted participation.

As early as 1929 it was proposed that the committee look into the matter of obtaining club premises. At the annual general meeting in 1930 it was proposed that the club purchase a hut as training quarters and clubrooms but an amendment that they should not entertain purchasing a hut, chiefly owing to the lack of funds, was carried. It was then moved that the club should have premises rented yearly or by lease, because of congestion at the Baths. The committee were instructed to make enquiries. The 1935 annual general meeting once again called for a hall for training. But all these enquiries came to no avail.

Cross-country club winners in the 1953-54 season. They are (standing, left to right)—R. Dryden (Jubilee Trophy); J. Jack (Junior Championship); W. Yule (Junior Cup); and R. Scott (Langheugh Trophy). Seated—J. Carruthers (Menzies Trophy); H. Lawrence (Campbell Trophy); and G. McDavid (Senior Cup).

In 1948, a special committee was formed to raise funds for the building of a clubroom in Bath Street but the refusal of a grant from the Playing Fields Association because the club did not hold a permanent lease of the site resulted in a series of delays.

Another big effort came in 1954 when a new committee was formed and this time building work was begun. It took two years to complete the work. Although local tradesmen carried out the main construction, the "donkey work" and site preparation including transporting materials from a demolished country mansion, was done by club members in their spare time. Prominent among these volunteers were Stan Reid, Archie Richardson, Willie Knox, George Turnbull, Jim March and H. "Paddy" Lawrence.

Every avenue was explored to keep costs down to a minimum. Bricks were obtained when some of the old air raid shelters in the town were being demolished and senior members spent many Sunday mornings cleaning the old cement from the bricks so that they could be used again. Piping and timber for the floors and doors were purchased from contractors who were demolishing an old mansion house between Morebattle and Kelso.

The money for the new premises was obtained from Sunday night concerts, dances, whists and raffles, as well as gifts and interest-free loans from ex-members and friends. Initially, some £300 was raised which was enough to start the ball rolling but it was estimated the building eventually cost over £600.

Having enough money was always the problem and often the amount of work done depended on what funds were available. Eventually the brickwork was done — but so was the money. The four walls stood for some time before another sub-committee was formed headed by Jake Douglas and Wat Gray who organised dances and a series of lucrative Sunday night jazz concerts in the Town Hall and it was the proceeds from these that provided the money for the roof. Some members by this time felt that the building was taking too long, was too big and using up too much of the club funds. So once more a special effort was organised which resulted in the building being made wind and watertight. However, not all functions were money-spinners. A dance was organised at Lilliesleaf but a snowstorm on the night prevented anyone from attending and the evening was a complete flop.

It was therefore a great day when the clubrooms were opened on 8th September, 1956, by Provost George Fraser and at the time few clubs in Scotland could boast better premises. The Provost said that the new hall was a fine example to the town of what could be done by the co-operative effort of individuals. It showed the achievement of constancy of purpose and demonstrated how wise and active members of the community could band together to overcome seemingly insurmountable difficulties. He congratulated members on their courage and energy in carrying out a job that could not have been accomplished without the zest they had brought to it.

The opening of the clubrooms was a great morale booster and signalled the run-up to a period in the 1960s when they enjoyed a fantastic spell of Eastern District dominance.

Seniors who took part in the 1959 Cup race at Hawick Moor.

Season 1959-60 opening run. The captain is Jim Jack (centre with dark sash).

INTER-CITY MEDALS SUCCESS

Teviotdale's first venture into the cross-country league came in the 1957-58 season in which their final placings were seniors fourth and juniors third. Best individuals for the Hawick club were H. Lawrence (seniors) 13th and K. Harley (juniors) second. In 1958 Teviotdale were the first Border club to be invited to send a team to the 44¼-mile Edinburgh to Glasgow road-relay race. Though they finished 17th from 20 clubs the Hawick runners were not discouraged and resolved to be better prepared for the following year's event. At their second attempt their fortunes went beyond expectations. In finishing a fantastic sixth, they were awarded medals as "the most meritorious unplaced team." The Teviotdale heroes and their individual placings and distances that day were:— K. Harley (2nd) 5½ miles; B. Mather (5th) 6 miles; J. Wood (3rd) 4 miles; G. Meikle (4th) 5¾ miles; J. Hamilton (5th) 5½ miles; J. Jack (6th) 7 miles; D. Campbell (6th) 5½ miles; R. Renton (6th) 5 miles.

The 1958-59 cross-country season also showed great improvement from Teviotdale runners. In the East league the seniors were second in each of the three races and the juniors were again third in the final placings. Throughout the league programme best performances came from seniors K. Harley (third); J. Jack (sixth) and B. Mather (seventh); while in the juniors C. Douglas was third on two occasions. In the Eastern District Championships that season the seniors were third. Then came the 1960s.

THE PHENOMENAL SUCCESSES OF THE 1960s

This decade in the club's history would require a book in itself to give it full justice and another would be required for a detailed account of the many individual performances during this period, especially those of Craig Douglas.

In the Eastern District cross-country senior championship, Teviotdale were runner-up in 1960 and 1961 to be followed in 1962 by taking the title — the first time by a club outwith Edinburgh and breaking a five-year run by Edinburgh Southern Harriers. Hawick counters that day were:— 3, Keith Harley; 4, Craig Douglas; 7, Brian Mather; 15, Jim Jack; 20, George Meikle; 25, Peter Roden. As Douglas was the first under 21-year-old to finish he was East of Scotland junior champion. The 1961 junior champion was Harley. In the 1963 championship, Craig was first to finish and though still only a 21-year-old, race officials refused to award both senior and junior trophies to the same runner. The

---

On facing page: 1959, the 75th anniversary year. Seniors and officials are:— back row (left to right)—S. Milligan, G. Meikle, B. Mather, D. Riddell, J. Newbigging, K. Harley, D. Mitchell, C. Douglas, R. Jeffrey. Middle row—W. Ferguson, G. Wright, W. Riddell, I. Deans, A. Oliver, S. Reid, V. Law (vice-president), J. Coltman, P. Roden. Front row—W. Yule, J. Jack (captain), G. Bell (hon. vice-president), G. Crawford (president), T. Burns (auditor), J. Hamilton (vice-captain and treasurer), D. Campbell (secretary).

CLUB
YS OF
SEPT
956

senior team finished third; the boys were also third with Raymond Nichol winning the individual title; and Joe Raeburn was runner-up in the youths' event. The following year the championships were held at Hawick and the host club's teams were in good form. With Joe Raeburn, 1st; Raymond Nichol, 4th; and George Moffat, 7th; the youths were first; and the seniors were runners-up with Craig Douglas, 4th; Keith Harley, 5th; Brian Mather, 11th; George Meikle, 15th; Peter Roden, 30th; John Hamilton, 42nd. In 1965, once again the seniors were second, the best of the individual placings being second from Craig Douglas.

The following year the senior boys were runners-up, with Ian Elliot individual champion, followed by Norman Taylor, 9th; and Michael Dodds, 13th. It was the turn of the junior boys in 1967 and they won the championship with John Marsh, 2nd; Murray Wilcox, 4th; and Hugh Petrie, 6th — some placings those — and in recognition of the support given by their team-mates, the club presented special medals to the other runners, namely: Derek Nicholson, Steven Lunn and Colin Hall. The 1968 Eastern District junior champion was Teviotdale's Gavin Richardson from Galashiels. In 1969 only two points denied the junior boys the title, their placings being: 3, Robert Hume; 5, Billy Darling; 10, Jim Blacklock.

Eastern District League races during the 1960s (there are three each season) were equally successful for Teviotdale.

In the 1960-61 season the final senior placing was runners-up, the second fixture being held at Hawick for the first time. Runners-up was also what the seniors had to be content with the following year, despite, for the first time ever, winning one of the fixtures. The win came from: 1, Craig Douglas; 4, Arthur Moody; 5, Brian Mather; 6, George Meikle; 10, Peter Roden; 24, Maxwell Telford. That same day the boys were also first with 2, Joe Raeburn; 3, David Henry; 7, Raymond Nichol but second in the final placings.

In 1962-63, the seniors started with a win and the youths were first equal but at the end of the season the seniors failed by only three points to win their first ever league title. Both youths and boys were runners-up, Joe Raeburn and Raymond Nichol respectively turning in the best placings. The following season second place once again went to both the seniors and youths. The final senior league placing in 1964-65 was again second, Craig Douglas being second in one and first in the other two. This was the season Craig ran two of the six miles in the third league race with only one shoe but still managed to breast the tape first.

The 1966-67 league programme started well for the junior boys. They won the first; then second at the next but remained on top and though they were runners-up again in the third race, they ended as the new league champions on points aggregate, to go into the history books as the first Teviotdale team to win an Eastern District league. During the season it was John Marsh (one first

Winners of the Kingsway Relay Trophy (Dundee) and McKenzie Trophy (Eastern District Relay Championship) in 1961. The team is (standing, left to right)—Arthur Moody and George Meikle, and (seated)—Craig Douglas and Brian Mather.

Winners of the Eastern District Cross-Country Senior Championships in 1962. The team is (standing, left to right)—Keith Harley, Peter Roden and Jim Jack, and (seated) Craig Douglas, Brian Mather and George Meikle.

and two seconds), Murray Wilcox, Steven Lunn and Derek Nicholson who made it possible.

The first league race in the 1968-69 season resulted in a win for the senior boys (John Marsh was third) and the junior boys were first equal (Billy Darling was runner-up) and though the junior boys finished second at the next venue they remained top of the league. The senior boys dropped to third. When it came to the final race, the junior boys put three into the first four to finish and so beat the much fancied Bathgate to lift the Teribus Cup which Teviotdale presented to the Eastern District in 1967. The heroes that day were:— 1, Billy Darling; 2, Robert Hume; 4, Jim Blacklock.

SCOTTISH CHAMPIONSHIPS

Only the juniors in 1961 won a Scottish team championship in the 1960s. They had been runners-up the season previously with: 6, Brian Mather; 7, Keith Harley; 24, Peter Roden; 25, George Meikle. In 1961 the team counters were: 4, Keith Harley; 7, George Meikle; 18, Peter Roden; 56, Dennis Riddell.

In 1962 the boys were runners-up (7, Joe Raeburn; 11, David Henry; 26, Billy Pearce; 30, Raymond Nichol) and again in 1966 (10, Tommy Dagg; 12, Michael Dodds; 21, Norman Taylor; 27, Ian Elliot).

The first time Teviotdale entered the Kingsway Relay at Dundee, that was October 1961, the team of Brian Mather, George Meikle, Arthur Moody, Craig Douglas, brought it to Hawick and this same quartet the following month lifted the McKenzie Trophy in the East of Scotland Cross-Country Relay Championship — the first time it had gone to a club other than from Edinburgh, Dundee or Aberdeen since Gala Harriers won in 1919, the year the event was inaugurated.

In March 1962 Teviotdale entered Edinburgh Southern's Fernieside relay for the first time and finished runners-up, then the McAndrew Relay at Glasgow in October and finished third from 70 teams. The combination of Craig Douglas, George Meikle, Peter Roden, and Brian Mather failed by only 15 yards to retain the Kingsway Trophy in the 1962-63 season but the quartet retained the East of Scotland Relay Championship from 22 teams; won the Hammarskjold Relay Trophy and ended the cross-country season by also winning the Fernieside Trophy.

For the 1963-64 cross-country programme, the relay squad was Craig Douglas, Brian Mather, Keith Harley and Roddy Wilson and once again Teviotdale were among the best in Scotland in this their 75th anniversary season. They were runners-up in the McAndrew Relay, then got their hands once more on the Kingsway Trophy and the McKenzie Trophy. While the seniors were sweeping all before them, Raymond Nichol, David Henry and Joe Raeburn won the youths' relay at the Lewisvale Spartans meeting — a trio which were to figure prominently in the years to come. With Douglas, Mather, Roden and Raeburn, the seniors were runners-up for the McKenzie Trophy in 1964-65 season and held the same placing the following season with Meikle replacing Roden.

Teviotdale's senior team who were runners-up to Edinburgh Southern in the 1964 Eastern District Cross-Country Championships staged at Hawick. The team, which includes three sets of brothers, is (back row, left to right)—George Meikle, Peter Roden, Alan Roden, Dennis Riddell, Billy Riddell. Front row—Andy Douglas, Craig Douglas, Keith Harley, Brian Mather, Rob Wharton.

Winners of the St Mungo Shield for the invitation medley relay at the Braw Lads' Gathering, Galashiels, in 1962. The team is (standing, left to right)—Dennis Riddell and Peter Roden, and (seated)—Craig Douglas and Andy Douglas.

Members and guests at the 1964 annual dinner.

In 1967 Hawick Burns Club donated a trophy to the Harriers. Pictured here is their club president J. Berridge presenting it to T. Dagg, the first winner.

Seniors prior to the 1962-63 season opening run. As well as the club trophies on display, in the centre is the St Mungo Shield, won in the relay at the Braw Lads Gathering, Galashiels. Seated front row centre is club president John Veitch and on his right is captain Brian Mather.

Border champions in 1960, Teviotdale Harriers included are: back row—I. Wear (third left) shot and discus; and J. Jack (extreme right) mile; front row—J. L. Coltman (second left) 100 yards and R. Renton (second right) 3 mile.

TRACK PROGRAMME

Even in the "glory days" of the 1960s, the successes over the cross-country could not be matched on the track in the contests during the summer months. There was plenty of individual talent but to win contests a club must have strength in depth and be able to cover all events. More often than not it was in the field events that Teviotdale dropped much-needed points.

In the 1960 club championships, Rob Renton set a new record of 2 mins. .08 secs. for the 880 yards. And it was in a match against Melrose in May 1961 that Peter Roden clocked 1:58.7 for a new club best and the first time a Teviotdale athlete had broken the 2-minute barrier. The following months in the club championships Roden reduced it to 1:57.2, then 1:56.2 in a league contest against Garscube at Hawick.

The mile is a popular event in any club and Teviotdale are no exception. During 1964 Roddy Wilson, a member from St Boswells, bettered the mile record three times within a month bringing K. Harley's 1961 time of 4 mins. 16.4 secs. down to 4:10.8.

In the 1964 track season, 24 Teviotdale athletes picked up 68 prizes. Their 55 handicap prizes included 21 firsts, and there were 10 Border titles, one Scottish title, one East of Scotland title and one East of Scotland ladies' title. The 1966 track season was even better with 80 prizes shared between 19 athletes. These included 42 handicap placings, 23 invitations or scratch prizes, three East of Scotland titles and 12 Border titles. Craig Douglas accounted for 23 of the total. Others picking up prizes and prominent in the inter-club contests during the '60s were track men Joe Raeburn (the first to break 15 mins. for the 3-mile, his 14:54.6 being set in 1963), Brian Mather, Peter Roden, Francis Cannon, Ian Elliot, George Meikle and Dennis Riddell, and field events specialists David Forrest, Ian Weir and even Hawick-born Olympic pole-vaulter David Stevenson, Edinburgh University, turned out for Teviotdale. Last but by no means least, there was David Henry from Galashiels who competed in the 880 yards. He won the Scottish youths' championship in 1963; the Scottish junior title in 1964—that was the year club-mates Kenny Oliver and Raymond Nichol finished second and third respectively; running for the S.A.A.A. against Atalanta in July 1964 Henry clocked 1 min. 54.6 secs. for a club junior record and the fastest by a junior in Scotland that year; and he reached international level in Scotland's match against East and West Midlands at Blackpool in September 1964.

In 1965 the club was presented with a new track trophy named the Coltman Challenge Cup but it was an award with a difference. This was not for any particular race and was open to all age groups. Former club sprint champion Jake Coltman donated the trophy to be presented annually to the "most outstanding track athlete of the season." The first recipient was Craig Douglas and over the years has gone to youngsters, seniors and ladies.

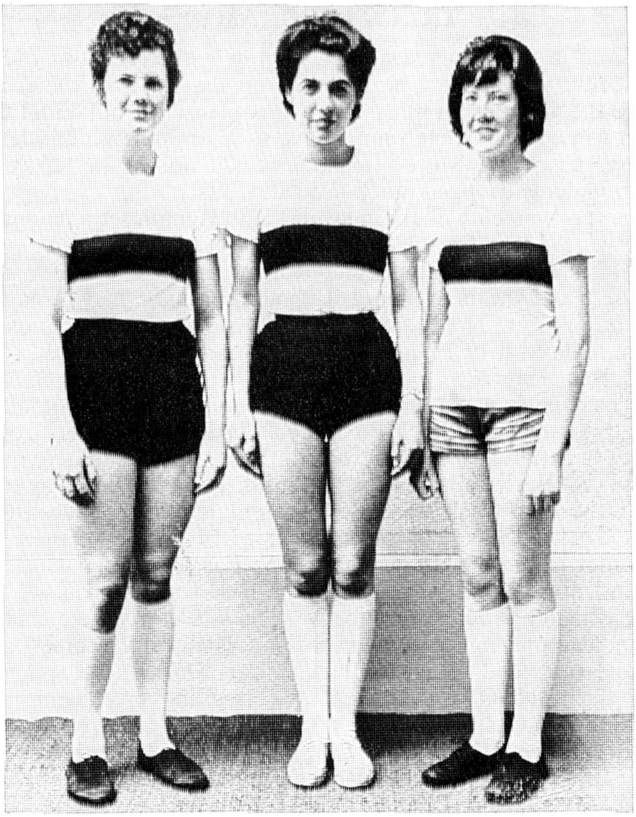

Scottish Intermediate Ladies Cross-Country Champions in 1965 (left to right)—Eleanor Petrie, Betty Jarvis and June Green.

Scottish Intermediate Ladies Cross-Country Champions in 1966 (left to right)—June Green, Eleanor Petrie and Anne Wilcox.

LADIES' SECTION

Turning the attention to the ladies' section, as has already been noted, this was formed in 1930 but their successes in open competition were few — that was until the 1960s. It was Mr and Mrs Kenny Borthwick, assisted by Mrs Marjory Hamilton, who reformed the section in 1961 and brought it back to popularity, having been disbanded five years earlier.

Looking at their track successes first, the most outstanding athletes were Eleanor Petrie and Betty Jarvis. In the 1963 East Championships, Betty picked up titles in the junior 100 and 150 yards and Eleanor was first in the junior long jump. The former went on to win the Scottish junior 100 yards title the following month. Eleanor retained her long jump title in 1964. The 1965 East Championships again had Teviotdale girls picking up medals. Eleanor won the intermediate 880 yards in 2 mins. 33.1 secs. — 20.3 secs. better than the senior winner; Margaret Fraser won the junior 150 yards; Pauline Murdoch was runner-up in the junior javelin; and Betty Jarvis was third in the intermediate 220 yards. Because of her win Eleanor was selected for the East team in the match against the West and she won the 880 yards in 2:22.2, a personal best by eight secs, and she also finished second in the 440 yards. In her first race as an intermediate, Anne Wilcox won the 880 yards title vacated by clubmate Eleanor. In the championships the following year, Eleanor retained her 880 title and made it a "double" by picking up the one-mile crown. On the same day, Jeanette Johnston won the junior 880 yards. The latter was picked for the East v. West match and the 13-year-old came in first.

No titles came to Teviotdale girls in the Scottish Women's A.A.A. Championships in 1967 but they did come so very close. Betty Jarvis, who had broken the 100 yards club record the previous month clocking 11.7 secs. (the previous best being C. Mactaggart's 11.9 in 1952) finished second in the 440 yards to Commonwealth Games athlete Rosemary Stirling, the Hawick girl's time being the second fastest recorded by a Scot that year. Eleanor Petrie was third in the 880; Anne Wilcox was second in the intermediate 880; Pauline Tucker was third in the 100 and Jeannette Johnston was third in the junior 880. With such talent, it came as no surprise when a team comprising Tucker (220), Wilcox (220), Jarvis (440) and Petrie (880) were runners-up in the Scottish one-mile medley relay championship in 1967.

As expected Eleanor Petrie was noticed by the Scottish selectors and she gained her first international "vest" in September 1967 running for her country in an inter-territorial match, clocking 2:25.9, her best time that year, for fourth place. The following track season, 1968, she repeated her 1967 "double" by winning both the 880 yards and mile and her subsequent selection for the East v. West match saw her finishing second in the 880 in a personal best of 2:22.0 — and this after being spiked during the race. The wound required four stitches.

In the period under review, the ladies' section were equally successful over the cross-country as they had been on the Scottish track scene.

Though only reformed in September 1961, within five months they finished third in the Scottish championships, the team being: 12, Ellen Newbigging; 14, Netta Scott; 16, Joan Scott; 17, Margaret Borthwick. The following year the club finished runner-up in the junior championship, the team that day being: 3, Eleanor Petrie; 8, June Green; 16, Elaine Nichol. They went one better in 1964 by winning the Scottish junior championship, by a margin of 14 points with the following team: 2, Petrie; 3, Green; 5, Wilcox. In the 1965 championships it was "gold" again for Teviotdale girls, this time at intermediate level with: 2, Petrie; 3, Green; 8, Jarvis. Wilcox, still a junior, was runner-up in her championship race. The intermediate Scottish title was retained the following year with Petrie finishing first and so gaining an individual national "crown," followed by: 7, Wilcox; 9, Green. In the girls' championship that day Teviotdale finished third with: 6, Jeanette Johnston; 7, Ann Little; 22, Carol Hall, Johnston being a name which was to figure greatly in Scottish cross-country circles within a year. For the sixth successive year the ladies' section excelled in the Scottish Championships. In 1967 Jeanette Johnston won the junior title; the girls' team were runners-up by one point with: 2, Ann Little; 4, Mary McHugh; 7, Margaret McHugh; and the intermediate team finished third with: 6, Anne Wilcox; 8, C. Balfour; 19, Joyce Aimers. The following year they were among the medals again with "silver" going to Ann Little, Jeanette Johnston and Margaret McHugh. In the months previous to the championship the trio had swept all before them but on that occasion Bathgate, beaten many times by the Hawick club, snatched the title.

Many other performances by the ladies' section must go on record. In the 1965 English Championships, Eleanor Petrie and June Green were third and eighth respectively and as they were not included in the official Scottish team, Teviotdale paid their expenses — and as it turned out — money well spent. The club was also represented in the 1968 English Championships and were the only Scottish team of their age group. The junior girls showed they were not out of their depth by finishing sixth from 26 clubs, the runners being: 17, Jeanette Johnston; 25, Margaret McHugh; 32, Ann Little; 52, Mary McHugh. Also in 1968 Eleanor Petrie gained a cross-country "vest" in the inter-area match. In the 1967 S.W.C.C.U. international trial Anne Wilcox was third, the first intermediate to finish, while in the other events, Ann Little (girls) and Jeanette Johnston (juniors) were first in their respective events. That season to February, Jeanette recorded firsts in every open race she entered as well as three club events.

The Borthwick Trophy, donated by Mr and Mrs Kenny Borthwick in 1964, was introduced for the ladies' championships.

Jeanette Johnstone, Scottish Junior Cross-Country Champion in 1967.

Club captain, cross-country club champion and top track athlete of 1976, Alison Campbell who emigrated to South Africa in 1979. She was a team member of a club known as Celtic Harriers who beat the South African women's 24-hour record of continuous mile relaying in 1981.

Andy Douglas winning the Senior Cup race in 1962.

Joe Raeburn, junior cross-country club champion 1962, 1963, 1964 and senior club champion 1967, 1969.

Prizewinners in the first Christie Cup race in 1964 pictured with Mrs Ella Scott who donated the trophy in memory of her father Robert Christie, a prominent Harrier who won the Cup in 1895, club championship in 1899 and 1900, and was captain from 1898 to 1901. The prizewinners are (left to right)— John Conroy (second), Grant Moyes (first) and Rob Wharton (third).

Bruce Millar, the first winner of the M. and M. Trophy in 1969 with the donors George Meikle (left) and Grant Moyes.

MEN'S SECTION

The years between 1960 and 1970 saw great performances at club level by such record-breakers as Brian Mather, Arthur Moody (both from Galashiels), Keith Harley and Joe Raeburn.

Their successes were on such a scale that space permits only a brief mention.

Cup Race, 1961—Moody broke the junior record by 11 secs. which had stood to W. Smith since 1934.

Menzies Trophy, 1961—Harley bettered the record by 19 secs.

Championship, 1961—Mather broke the senior record by 73 secs.

Langheugh Trophy, 1962—New record by Mather by 82 secs.

Championship, 1962—Raeburn broke the junior record by 40 secs.

Menzies Trophy, 1963—Harley broke his own record by 37 secs.

Milestones in the club's history during the period under review were many, here are just some of them.

In 1962 Teviotdale runners tackled the Ben Nevis race for the first time, finishing fourth from 21 teams with Maxwell Telford, John Hamilton and George Meikle. The last named was to compete in the Eildon Hill race over the years winning more times than anyone can remember. It is 10 at the moment according to George and his running days are not over yet!

The Christie Cup was presented in 1964 by Mrs G. D. Scott, Summerfield, in memory of her father, Rob Christie, a prominent Harrier of the 1900s. The first holder of the trophy for the 2¼-mile race was Grant Moyes.

It was George Meikle and Grant Moyes who presented the M. & M. Trophy for a junior boys' one-lap event on Cup Race day. That was 1969 and the first holder was Bruce Millar.

Cup Race 1965 was the biggest day's programme tackled to date with five events at the Moor, such was the strength of the membership. It was around 140 at that time. That day Billy Riddell retained the Senior Cup, an achievement no other Harrier had accomplished since the event was instituted in 1894 or has done to the present day. It is interesting to note that it was his younger brother Dennis who won in 1966.

Jubilee Trophy race day in November 1965 is one the Petrie family will remember with pride. Sixteen-year-old Eleanor, 13-year-old Hazel and 11-year-old Hugh "swept the boards" by taking first place in the events for ladies, girls and boys respectively.

The first Hawick Burns Club Trophy race for boys aged 11-17 years was in 1966 and so began an association which has continued to the present day and further sponsorship came from the Burns Club in 1976 when they presented the Will Clark Memorial Trophy for competition among seniors. Mr Clark had taken a great interest in the local Harriers.

Track and cross-country internationalist Craig Douglas.

CRAIG DOUGLAS

Attention must now be centred on the outstanding career of Craig Douglas. To do him justice the remainder of this book would have to be devoted to him but that is not possible. Craig will surely understand.

As well as his contribution to Teviotdale's successes in open competition already mentioned, Craig's record-breaking performances at club level and his international appearances have never been matched by any other club member. He bettered every senior cross-country club record with the exception of the Cup Race, that was one that always eluded him.

The first to fall was the junior championship in 1961 when he smashed Dennis Riddell's 1959 time by 32 secs; that was followed by the senior championship by 27 secs. in 1962; the Jubilee record by 13 secs. the same year; the Jubilee by 10 secs. in 1963; the club championship by 12 secs. in 1964; the Jubilee by 5 secs. again in 1964; the Christie Cup record in 1964, another 3 secs. off that the following year and another 18 secs. in 1966; the Langheugh record was shattered by 51 secs. in 1965; and that year the Menzies went to him by 6 secs.

Craig's international cross-country career started in 1962 when, along with clubmate Arthur Moody, they were members of Scotland's junior team in the international championships at Sheffield. The following year he was again in the junior team this time in the European Championships in Spain when he finished 10th and he was in the Scotland v. British Army match in 1964, finishing sixth, and 1966, finishing 18th.

His track career both as an internationalist and club runner was what really made him well known not only in his home town but much further afield as well. He was a force to be reckoned with over any distance from 100 yards to 3 miles, as shown by his Border championship titles listed elsewhere but it was in the half-mile that he will best be remembered.

In 1963, two months after winning the Scottish 880 yards championship in 1 min. 55.2 secs., he was second in the 880 in the match between Home Scots and Anglo Scots and second in the match against Belgium. The East of Scotland title was his in 1964 in a new championship record of 1:54.8; the following month he finished first against Sweden in 1:53.3—a club record.

In May 1965 he retained his East crown, again setting a new championship record at 1:53.5; and then the following month his time of 1:51.7 in winning the 880 in the Scotland v. Atalanta (combined Scottish universities) match was not only a club record, it was the fastest in Scotland that year and only one second outside the national record. In July 1965 he clocked a record 1:50.0 in the match against Midland Counties and Wales at Birmingham but that was not ratified as an official national record as it had been done outside Scotland. That time was the tenth equal fastest in

Craig Douglas winning the Eastern District Cross-Country League race at Hawick in 1965—having run the last two of the six-mile event with only one shoe!

Britain for 1965. The following month Craig was second in the match against Ireland. He began his 1966 track season — a year he will never forget — with a club record of 4 mins. 10.7 secs. in the pre-Cup Final invitation mile at Hampden; retained the East 880 title for the third successive time; and in the Scotland v. Midlands v. Wales match, finished within three tenths of a second from G. Dean who ran for Britain in the Tokyo Olympics. June 1966 saw him winning the 880 for the S.A.A.A. against Atalanta, keeping his personal record of not being beaten by a Scottish half-miler that season, then the following month, competing against the English Midlands, South and Wales, finished first in 1:49.9, at the time the fastest ever by a Scot — but again not ratified by the S.A.A.A. who are reluctant to recognise records done outside Scotland. A national record was again in his sights in the invitation 1000 yards at Edinburgh Highland Games that year. Finishing third, ahead of a Kenyan who was a Commonwealth Games silver medalist, Craig equalled the national record with 2 mins. 10.9 secs.

It is obvious from the performance related that Craig travelled the length and breadth of Britain to compete in prestige events, an example being in August 1966 when he covered a distance of 1000 miles within three days. That was Cowal Games, Dunoon, on the Friday and Northampton the following day. At the former his win in a special invitation 880 in 1:51.1 was the highlight of the meeting. That day there was a new kind of prize for amateurs. Cigarette gift coupons were given by the sponsors in place of the usual trophies and prizes so that the successful athletes could choose their own gifts. Craig received 5000 for his win. Also on offer were 10,000 coupons if the Scottish record was broken — Craig's time was only eight-tenths of a second outside. On the Saturday he was in Northampton competing in the one-mile and in this reduced the 1964 club record of 4:10.8 held by R. Wilson to 4:9.7. Some weekend indeed! The following month Craig was competing against Munich, again winning, this time the 800 metres and he also had the distinction of carrying the Scottish flag in the closing ceremony.

In December 1966, Craig made his debut on boards at the Wolverhampton indoor stadium, striking "gold" once more in the 880 yards and then two months later in the British indoor championships he finished fourth in the final after knocking out the reigning champion in the heats.

In May 1967 following what was described at the time as an "internal dispute" Craig resigned from Teviotdale Harriers and joined Edinburgh Southern. This is no place to dicuss the "whys and wherefors" of the row, suffice to say that Teviotdale lost the services of a great athlete, the like of whom they will probably never see again — but, who knows, new talent is forever coming forward. Craig's international career continued with his new club until his retirement from competition in 1977 following a leg operation.

YOUNGSTERS IN THE LIMELIGHT — 1970-80

It was the turn of the girls, junior boys and senior boys' cross-country teams to steal the limelight in the period 1970-80.

Junior boys Derek Campbell, 3rd; Philip Nichol, 4th and Andrew Oliver, 15th, gave Teviotdale second place in the 1970 Eastern District Championships, then they finished fourth in the Scottish Championships that year — the first East team. That form was carried into the 1970-71 season with the league programme finishing with Teviotdale junior boys runners-up. Oliver had the best placings — 3rd, 2nd and 6th.

In the 1971-72 season, open race wins were recorded by a young Teviotdale Harrier who was eventually to be included in

Bill Riddell breasts the tape in the Hawick R.F.C. Sevens mile handicap in 1963.

John Marsh celebrating his win in the boys' handicap at the 1967 Hawick R.F.C. Sevens.

Scotland's 1986 Commonwealth Games team. That was Colin Hume. Colin and clubmates David Hall and Stuart Wilkinson won the first junior boys' league race in the 1972-73 season; they finished second in the next and so did the senior boys; then both sections ended the league programme runners-up. The Eastern District Championships that season saw both the junior and senior boys in third place, the runners being:— junior boys: 2, Colin Hume; 9, Stuart Wilkinson; 14, David Hall. Senior boys: 17, Kenny Hill; 22, Robert Pendreigh; 30, David Anderson. The 1973-74 season was an even better one for the junior boys who finished first in all three league races to win the Teribus Trophy which the Hawick club had donated to the East District several years previously. The team counters were:— Hume, Michael Veitch and Wilkinson, then they went on and carried off the Eastern District Championship, Hume finishing first and so became the individual champion, followed by Veitch, 5th and Brian Neilson, 6th. They ended the season finishing fourth in the Scottish Championships, Colin being runner-up. It came as no surprise therefore when Colin set a new record in the club's boys' championship and the M. and M. Trophy race that season and again in the boys' championship in 1974.

The cross-country season 1974-75 was another successful one for the junior boys who ended the league programme in second place, thanks to some fine performances by Steven Hogg and Drew Lauder. It was Hogg who clipped one second off Hume's record in the boys' club championship that season.

The 1975-76 season was an even better one for Teviotdale with the senior boys taking the honours this time. Showing complete dominance at this level, the Hawick club was 22 points ahead after the first fixture, 70 after the second and then won the third to top the Eastern District League with 86 points from Edinburgh A.C. on 185 and Falkirk 222. Their placings that season were so good that they deserve to be given in detail:—1st race: 1, Colin Hume; 5, Brian Neilson; 11, John Darling; 16, Steven Hogg. 2nd race: 1, Neilson; 3, Hume; 13, Darling; 15, Hogg. 3rd race: 1, Neilson; 2, Hume; 6, Darling; 12, Hogg. The junior boys started their league programme runners-up in the first fixture (4, Drew Lauder; 10, Brian Hume; 14, Richard Smith; 15, Stuart McCrone) but ended in fourth place.

The senior boys went on to make it a "double" by winning the Eastern District Championship and with it the Edinburgh A.C. Cup, by 13 points from Central Region (22) and Falkirk (33). Colin Hume finished first that day in January 1976 to make him East champion, with clubmates Neilson and Darling 2nd and 10th respectively. In the Scottish Championships the following month the boys came so near to winning the title. Teviotdale's 68 points were only four behind Victoria Park, Central Region trailed on 80. The senior boys' placings were:— 2, Hume; 5, Neilson; 24, Darling; 37, Hogg.

Teviotdale junior boys in season 1973-74, winners of all three Eastern District League races, the Eastern District Championship and fourth in the Scottish Championship.

Teviotdale senior boys in season 1975-76, winners of all three Eastern District League races and the Eastern District Championship. They are (standing, left to right)—J. Darling, and S. Hogg, and (seated) B. Neilson and C. Hume. Hume is holding the Tom D. Todd Trophy which he won as the individual champion.

Juniors and ladies' section season 1968-69 opening run.

The ladies' section opening run of the 1976-77 season.

Acting Burns Club president H. Spreng, with Burns Club Trophy winner R. Smith and Will Clark Memorial Trophy winner A. Oliver in 1977.

A group of the 1971-72 season's trophy winners.

NEW TROPHIES

In this 10-year period under review, Teviotdale were presented with a number of new trophies for club competition.

The Craig Douglas Trophy was gifted by him for competition in the ladies' section in 1971. Originally for the 100 yards, it was later changed to the 300 metres, then 200 metres and now is for the 100 metres championship.

Along with his brother Andy, the Douglas Trophy was presented in 1975 for the girls' championship.

The Ladies' Challenge Trophy for competition at the Moor on Cup race day was donated by club member Alison Campbell in 1979 prior to her emigrating to South Africa.

In 1979 came the Erskine Trophy (senior championship sealed handicap) donated by Mrs Erskine whose late husband Dave held the title 1922-26; the Burnfoot Residents' Association Trophy (junior boys on Langheugh Trophy race day); and also on that day, but for girls, the Lodge III Trophy and for junior, youths and boys, another Lodge III Trophy. Lodge members expressed a wish to support activities for youngsters in the town. Mr W. Aimers donated the Glencairn Trophy in 1980 for the first "veteran" (over 40 years) to finish in the Cup race. It was on 15th September, 1930, that the ladies of Hawick first took to cross-country running and

Some of the season's prizewinners at the annual dinner in 1977.

the captain who led the pack that day, Betty White, was present at the Bath Street clubrooms in September 1980 when their Golden Jubilee was celebrated with a special club run. In January 1981, Miss White presented them with a trophy to be known as the Ladies' Jubilee Trophy.

GIRL INTERNATIONALISTS

Success in this period was not confined to the male members in the club, the "fair sex" enjoyed an equally successful run of achievements.

Pauline Cairns was one of only 40 Scots girls chosen for the S.W.C.C. League team to run against the English regions in 1978. The 14-year-old was in record-breaking form in March 1979. Competing in the junior event at the Annan "River Races" she broke the course record by 25 secs. which had been set several years previously by Barbara Geddes, also Teviotdale. Not only that, Pauline's time was faster than the senior event over the same course and came despite falling heavily 800 metres out. That same month and just 15, she was fourth in the Scottish Schools' Championship and 15th in the British Schools' Championship and this with her at the younger end of the 15-17 years age group. At the start of the 1979-80 cross-country season Pauline won the East District intermediate title, again against 15-17-year-olds and in the December both Pauline and Gillian Renwick were worthy recipients of an international "vest" running in the four Home Countries' International at Bolton (Pauline was 24th; Gillian, the second Scot in her age group, was 12th). Following this Pauline was selected for the S.W.C.C.U. team for the Five Nations Cross-Country International at Runcorn, Cheshire, in which she was 24th, the third Scot. In the 1980 Scottish Championships she finished third. While most of Pauline's successes were in cross-country events, she did win the 1980 East 800 metres in a personal best time to add a track title to her many achievements. During her running days Pauline set several cross-country club records includ-

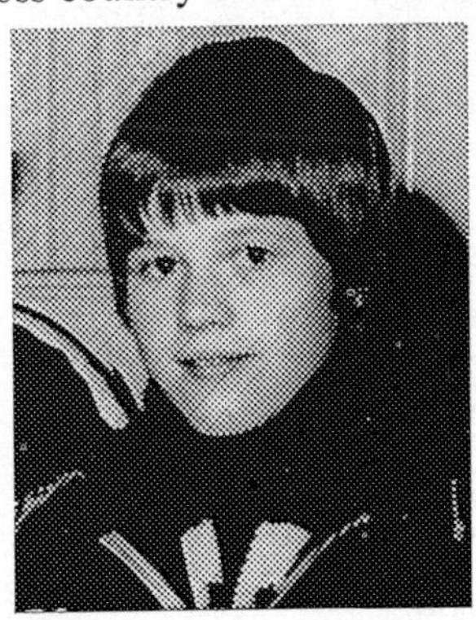

Cross-country internationalists Pauline Cairns (left) and Gillian Renwick.

ing the 1976 girls' championship; 1979 ladies' championship; Ladies' Challenge Trophy race in 1979 and 1981, the latter by 40 secs.; 1980 Lodge III Trophy race; and Ladies' Jubilee Trophy race in 1981.

Before moving from girls, further mention must be made of Gillian Renwick who won the Douglas Trophy (girls' club championship) in a new record time in 1980; and not forgetting the record-breaking win by Barbara Geddes in the 1974 ladies' championship for the Borthwick Trophy; the new record set by Shona Cumming winning the 1979 Douglas Trophy; and Diane Yellowlees winning the 1980 minor girls' championship, taking 30 secs. off the record in the process.

Finally, there was the 1971 club dinner which 13-year-old Margaret Oliver will never forget. She was presented with the S.W.C.C.U. Certificate of Merit for her performance, which was 6th, in the national championships. The certificate arrived only hours before the start of the dinner and only two or three officials knew of the surprise presentation.

Being on the subject of social activities, one of the most enjoyable nights was in October 1971 when Teviotdale organised a re-union for ex-members. Over 80 guests were present among them 78-year-old Jimmy Grierson, 80-year-old Tommy Hamilton and 85-year-old Jim Telfer. Jock Carruthers will remember the 1973 dinner with pride as he received the President's Medal in recognition of his services to the club as a former president, eight years as ladies' secretary and 15 years as committeeman. The medal was originally presented by the 1932 president, Tom Gillies, for annual recognition of various athletic achievement.

Above—Angela Bennett, the top athlete of 1978, won the club's senior title at 300 metres and junior title at 800 metres that year and was the first holder of the Ladies' Jubilee Trophy in the 1980-81 cross-country season. She was captain in the 1979-80 season.

(Right)
First winner of the Lodge 111 Trophy for the intermediate/ senior ladies race in 1979 was Denise Irvine.

The 1977-78 opening run of the cross-country season. Captain John Murray is seated third from left.

The ladies' section jubilee was celebrated in 1980 with a special run when Miss White, captain in 1930, was the guest.

In 1976, Hawick Lodge St. James B.U.R.A. No. 424 donated a trophy for the club's open races. The W.G.R. Memorial Trophy, in memory of the late W. G. Robertson, D.F.C., M.A., J.P., a Past Master of the Lodge, was handed over by R.W.M. G. Thomson (left) to Harriers president J. M. Hamilton.

At this stage in Teviotdale's history, few Saturday afternoons could be devoted to official club runs owing to the hectic programme of open and club competitions.

The following are some of the many team successes in the 1970-80 period:

1971—Second in the Carnethy Hill race with J. Marsh, R. Hume, W. Darling, B. Millar. A team took part in the Allan Scally Memorial relay for the first time, finishing 47th from 70 teams.

1975—In the Ben Nevis race all four Harriers gained standard

W. "Barty" Yule, winner of the Senior Cup in 1955, 1968, 1970 and 1973—a feat unequalled in the history of this, the oldest cross-country race in Scotland.

time certificates, awarded to those finishing within 3½ hrs. they were:— 47, John Marsh; 56, George Meikle; 94, Brian Gibson; 122, Tom Hutton. Marsh was second in the under 23-year-old section, his time of 1 hr. 51 mins. 38 secs. breaking the club best by six mins. previously held by Alan Samuel.

1980—In the Annan "River Races" team prizes were picked up by colts (3, Chris Murphy; 4, David Rudkin; 11, Michael Bryson) and intermediate/senior women (2, Pauline Cairns; 7, Nancy McCraw; 8, Angela Bennett). The Eyemouth 6-mile road-race was won (3, Brian Emmerson; 4, Ronnie Rodgins; 7, Stuart Bennett) and in that event Jim Bouglas was first "veteran" and Norman Taylor first novice. The St Mungo Shield for the men's relay at the Braw Lads' gathering came to Teviotdale with Francis Cannon, Neil Dalgetty, Neil Anderson and Derek Clyne.

Such were the many individual achievements during the 1970-80 period, space permits only brief details.

In this decade club records tumbled at a regular pace and as well as those already mentioned, six went to Ian Elliot. It took until March 1971 for Craig Douglas's 1964 championship record to fall, this went to Ian by four secs.; the same month he clipped eight secs. off the 11-year-old Senior Cup race record held by Jim Jack; in 1975 Ian broke his own Cup race record by 34 secs.; in 1976 he smashed the Craig Douglas Jubilee Trophy record of 12 years' standing by 55 secs.; the Menzies Trophy record the following season also went to Ian by 29 secs., another held by Craig; and in 1970 the 1500 metres best time of 4:17.3 was his.

The biggest improvement on a club record was in 1979 when, only weeks after being reinstated an amateur, Martin Elsdon bettered the championship record by a massive 1 min. 13 secs.

The junior championship record fell to Alastair Taylor by 1 min. 4 secs. in 1970; to John Marsh by 44 secs. in 1971 and to Brian Turnbull by 44 secs. in 1973.

Andrew Oliver bettered the time for the M. & M. Trophy in 1970 and 1971; and Drew Lauder set a new record in the 1973 colts' championship.

On the track, the 100 yards club championship, with a record of 10.4 secs. held jointly by Ian Bell (1958), Jake Coltman (1959) and Ian Dirom, Annan, (1964), was changed to metric in 1970 with Francis Cannon clocking 11.9 secs., only to be bettered by Duncan McGibbon from Selkirk in 1971—11.6 secs. and 1972—11.4 secs., and 1974 saw the start of an impressive run of successes with Brian Gibb winning the club title 12 times in 14 years. Brian's father George held the sprint title in 1953. Still on the track, Derek Clyne was awarded the trophy donated by club patron Dick Wilkinson for scoring most points in Scottish Young Athletes League fixtures in 1975 and the following year's winner was Drew Lauder. In the 1973 East of Scotland Championships, Ian Glendinning, from Langholm, won the junior 200 metres title in 22.9 secs. which was inside both the junior and senior standard

Above—
Alan Samuel, holder of the senior cross-country club championship in the five successive years from 1973.

Right—
Brian Gibb, 12 times winner of the club's 100 metres championship, pictured with the Scott Trophy. His run of successes started in 1974.

times as well as the national junior standard. In the Scottish Championships Ian was runner-up in the junior 100 metres.

Between 1970 and the early 1980s, there were few really outstanding team results in Teviotdale's track programme.

Their first participation in the Scottish Young Athletes' League was in 1973, finishing fourth and the following year the junior boys/senior boys/ youths were again fourth with the colts runners-up.

In 1978 Teviotdale moved to the Edinburgh and District Track League with some measure of success. In one match that year they won 17 events, "doubles" coming from Pauline Cairns (junior ladies) and Neil Anderson (senior men). In another match 10 events were won with "double" winners being Neil Dalgetty (youths) and Francis Cannon and Derek Clyne (both senior men). In the following season the club finished second in the Edinburgh and District League and fourth in the Scottish and North West League.

By 1980 athletics in the Borders was on the increase with clubs such as Melrose A.C. and Blackhill Harriers attracting a good following. In a match in which Teviotdale were hosts to the other Border clubs, the Hawick club finished first in more than half the events.

In 1980 is was back to the Edinburgh and District League with Teviotdale athletes recording several personal bests but the most outstanding were Chris Murphy who set a league record in the colts' 800 metres for the third time that season and Angela Bennett who gained her second league record of the season in the intermediate 800 metres. The following year Teviotdale tasted a brief spell of glory by finishing runners-up in the league and so gaining promotion to Division II for the 1982 season. In the final match the senior men won every track event but one to take first place and the women were runners-up, their joint score being enough to give them second place. Wins were recorded by senior men Stuart Barker, Brian Gibb and Neil Dalgetty and women Joanne McLeod, Angela Bennett, Pauline Cairns and Nancy McCraw. However, their success was short lived. At the end of the 1983 track season Teviotdale were relegated.

Turning again to the cross-country, the 1973 club senior championship was won by Alan Samuel, the start of what was to be a run of five successive titles, and winning the senior Cup that year gave W. "Barty" Yule four wins in the race, his other successes being 1955, 1968 and 1970.

Sponsorship became a feature of athletics on a national scale and Teviotdale were an obvious choice for Hawick's world famous knitwear firms. Peter Scott took over the Jubilee Trophy race in 1979, Pringle of Scotland first sponsored the Menzies Trophy race in 1980 and the Cup race was taken by Lyle and Scott the same year. Sponsorship of the cross-country club championships was taken up by Mitchells, the Hawick glazing firm, in 1981 and in 1985 Hawick Ex-Servicemen's Club presented a new trophy for the colts' championship and then took over sponsorship of this event. These local donors have continued sponsorship ever since for which the Harriers are indeed grateful.

UNUSUAL AWARDS

Surely the most unusual award ever gained by the Harriers was in 1972 when the seniors won a cross-country team event at Penicuik. They came home with a four-foot-long wrought-iron claymore. The team that won the Claymore Trophy was George Meikle (10th), Alan Samuel (11th) and Willie Lindsay (24th). Lindsay was also runner-up in the veterans' section and to complete a highly successful day, Teviotdale took firsts in the events for juniors and junior boys with John Marsh and Kenny Hill respectively.

Another strange prize was that gained by John Fairgrieve. While on a business trip to Hong Kong in 1976, he competed in a 6-mile road-race along with 400 Chinese and 10 Europeans. The main problem was the heat, 85°F. and the 95% humidity but John still managed to finish 13th for which he received a plaque, "suitably" inscribed — in Chinese!

Ian Jackson, Lyle & Scott promotions manager, congratulates winners in the Cup races first sponsored by the world famous knitwear company in 1980. They are (back row, left to right)—Joanne McLeod, Kevin Pringle and Francis Cannon, and (front row)—Chris Murphy and Brenda Liddle.

Harriers president Ronnie Pringle accepts the Ex-Servicemen's Club Trophy from the president, Doug Solley. The trophy was donated in 1984 for the colts' club championship.

COMMON-RIDING GAMES

When the Hawick Common-Riding Friday Amateur Games were shelved in 1961, Teviotdale Harriers took it upon themselves to sponsor the meeting. They were able to keep the Games going as an evening attraction for 10 years and in that time brought the cream of British athletes to the town.

The Games of 1964 had a 2-mile event as the main attraction. First was John Anderson (9 mins. 1 sec.), the British champion over the distance and though there were six English internationalists in the field, Teviotdale's Roddy Wilson (9:26.9) finished 4th, the best ever time by a club member.

A memorable year was 1966. After competing for Britain in Paris, Craig Douglas arrived home an hour before the start of the invitation mile and despite two Olympic athletes in the line-up, the local runner stole the show—even though he was only second. John Whetton, A.A.A., a Tokyo Olympics finalist was first in 4 mins. 17.3 secs., followed by Craig (4:13.5), with former Scottish champion Ken Ballantyne (4:17.2) third. Also in the field were Derek Ibbotson, A.A.A., Melbourne Olympics finalist and former world record-holder, and Hugh Barrow, the Scottish record-holder.

The greatest line-up of milers ever seen in the Borders was in the 1965 Games when 11 top-class athletes were invited. They were Alan Simpson, Olympic finalist, British mile champion and U.K. record holder at one mile, 1500 metres and 2000 metres; Derek Ibbotson; John Whetton, British indoor mile champion for three years; S. Taylor, former British mile champion; Hugh Barrow; Ken Ballantyne; Roddy Wilson, R.A.F. and Teviotdale record-holder; Ian McCafferty, later to win a medal for Scotland in the 1970 Commonwealth Games in Edinburgh; and Brendan Foster, Gateshead, who was to become one of the greats in British athletics. The result was Simpson, 4:3.7; Whetton, 4:4.4; Barrow, 4:6.0.

Several times during this period Hawick Common-Riding Committee were approached with a request for the Saturday on alternate years but every time this was turned down in favour of the Professional Games.

TWENTY YEARS OF OPEN RACES

It was 1968 that Teviotdale Harriers staged the first of what was to become very successful open cross-country races. In fact the fixture is now recognised as one of the top events in the Scottish calendar with Olympic and Commonwealth Games athletes taking part over the years.

That November afternoon in 1968 attracted 100 boys and girls for six events in the 11-15 years age group. By 1971 this had reached 300 in eight races and the "Hawick News" had kindly donated the first trophy. The following year 18 clubs came to Hawick making it the biggest cross-country fixture for youngsters in Scotland. In 1975 there were 750 runners and, because of this increased entry, the age group was now 9-17 years. That year Wilton Ward Association presented a trophy; two more followed in 1976, the Dave Scott Trophy from the S.B.A.A.A. president; and Lodge 424 gifted the W. G. R. Trophy in memory of the late Bill Robertson, one of their office-bearers.

Olympic athlete Linsey Macdonald, from the Pitreavie club in Dunfermline, was the "star" attraction in 1980 and 1981 when up to 50 clubs were now making the trip to Hawick to compete in nine events. The Army Careers Shield was donated in 1981; the Roy Jeffrey Memorial Shield was presented in 1982 by former Harrier Jim Hogarth in memory of his brother-in-law, also a former Harrier, who was tragically killed in a road accident; and the same year a trophy was presented by the Roxburgh District Sports Council. Trophies in all nine events came in 1984 with the Stan Reid Memorial Trophy, presented by Mrs Reid in memory of her late husband, a life-long member of the club; and the George Howden Scott Trophy, donated by the 1923-24 club captain's two sons. By 1984 the entry had reached 1000, representing clubs from all over Scotland and the North of England

Competition in the events over the years has been such that Teviotdale teams have only had nine wins since the start in 1968. Individual "firsts" have come from Billy Darling, junior boy, 1968; Colin Hume, colt, 1970, 1971 and junior boy, 1973; Martin Elsdon, senior, 1979; Chris Murphy, colt, 1980, 1981 and junior boy, 1982; and Alastair Walker, senior, 1984.

Teviotdale girls in the club's cross-country open races in November 1978.

Hawick's Wilton Lodge Park makes a perfect setting for Teviotdale's open races. Up among the leaders in the 1986 ladies' race is Joan Anderson of Teviotdale (no. 645).

Teviotdale girls in the 1987 Open Races at Hawick.

The senior men, including a large contingent from Teviotdale, in the 1987 Open Races at Hawick. Bill Knox (No. 758) was first to finish for the host club in 10th place.

SUCCESSES GALORE FROM 1980 TO CENTENARY YEAR

The finale decade in this history of Teviotdale Harriers saw continued successes both on the track and over the cross-country from teams and individuals. The majority of these successes came from the younger members of the club and it was not until the 1986-87 cross-country season that the senior men emulated the achievements of their club-mates of the 1960s.

A further five trophies were presented. In memory of her late husband who was a keen follower of athletics, Mrs D. Elliot presented the John Elliot Trophy in 1981 for competition among minor girls and girls on Cup race day; the Ex-Servicemen's Club donated a trophy in 1984 for the colts' championship; the Lodge St James 424 Trophy for senior boys and youths on Jubilee Trophy race day was presented in 1985; and that same year the Fire Brigade Cup was donated by the Hawick contingent for the minor girls and girls on Langheugh Trophy race day. Ironically, it was Colette Livingstone, daughter of one of the firemen, who was the first winner. In 1987 Refuge Assurance donated a trophy for competition among junior and senior boys over a 3000 metres course.

Between 1980 and the start of the centenary season (1988-89) so many successes came Teviotdale's way, it is difficult to know where to begin.

TRACK PROGRAMME

On the track outstanding successes were few but, of course, Teviotdale has always been a much stronger cross-country club.

In the 1981 Scottish and North West League, the Hawick club were in Division III and both the ladies and senior men were never out of the top three team placings. In the final match the men won every event but one, and in another Angela Bennett and Shona Cumming between them scored 62 points competing in six and five events respectively. The most outstanding during the season were Muriel Douglas, Pauline Cairns, Stuart Barker, Paul Robertson, Chris Murphy, Brian Gibb and Brian Emmerson. With results such as that, it was promotion for Teviotdale the following year. In subsequent years it was mixed fortunes for Teviotdale in the league, often winning as many as 12 events but still not having the backup to amass much-needed points. There appeared to be plenty of talent in depth in 1986 when 20 events were won in April and 30 in July to head Division IV and with a tremendous turn-out in September they finished on top by 200 points to gain promotion once again to Division III for 1987. Highlight of the 1987 league programme was T.H.C. winning 16 events in one fixture to win the men's match and finish third in the ladies.

Inter-club contests among the Border towns started in earnest in the 1980s and in the initial stages Teviotdale was too strong for the rest. An example of that was shown in August 1981 when the club won 22 events against Blackhill (Earlston), Melrose, Duns, Berwick and Tweedside (Kelso). A Borders Athletics League was formed but with it Blackhill and Melrose grew in stature and are now a force to be reckoned with. At the present time this pair can often outpoint Teviotdale on the track but they have virtually no winter club for cross-country events.

One Borders fixture which Teviotdale has really stamped its name on is the inter-club match for the Andrew Brown Memorial Trophy. It was presented in 1984 by the Galashiels Ex-Braw Lads' and Lasses' Association for annual competition. T.H.C. brought it back to Hawick in 1984, 1985, 1986 and 1987!

Deserving mention are the many track athletes who have sported a Teviotdale vest in open competition in the period under review.

In 1983 Brian Emmerson recorded his fourth successive win in the Black Hill race at Earlston. Then in 1985, Brian won the inaugural Manderston to Eyemouth half-marathon and the 6-mile Penicuik to Howgate road-race, the latter in a new course record; he also won the following year. Keith Elliot won the Eden half-marathon at Melrose in 1985 and David Cavers won the 15,000 metres Moffat road-race. Duns Sports has always been a "happy hunting ground" for Hawick athletes, as an example, in 1985 and 1986 Teviotdale athletes "swept the boards." In the 1985 Sports, firsts were recorded by Angela McClure (100 metres and 200 metres); Judith Murray (800 metres); Lynn Martin (shot); Neil Dalgetty (100 metres and 200 metres); Derek Clyne (800 metres); and the 6½-mile Law race was won by David Cavers, with club-mates Alex Renwick and Andy Fair backing well to lift the team prize. The Sports in 1986 showed a similar dominance with firsts from Keith Logan (800 metres and 1500 metres); Francis Cannon (200 metres); Judith Murray (800 metres); and Brian Emmerson (Law race). In May 1987, Teviotdale won the team prize in the 10-kilometre race at Penicuik with: 1, Alastair Walker; 3, Brian Emmerson; 15, Andy Fair. The follofing month (Brian Neilson (9th); Bill Knox (10th) and John Marsh (13th) were runners-up in the team race in the Eildon Two Hill Race at Melrose. Also that year, Rob Hall, a member from Jedburgh and a former "ped" who had been reinstated in the S.A.A.A. amnesty in the spring of 1986, was selected for the Scottish team in the Aberdeen Marathon. He finished a creditable third and the first counter in the national team.

NEW ALL-WEATHER BORDERS TRACK

The most important occasion in the Borders in 1984 was the opening of the new £225,000 all-weather track at Tweedbank, Galashiels, following months of controversy over its siting. Teviotdale was the first club to apply for use of the excellent facilities and that year switched the club championships to the new much needed stadium. This move delighted the other District Councils in the Borders following their differences with Roxburgh District as to why the track was not built in Hawick — the heartland of athletics in the area. The Hawick championships are now staged annually at Tweedbank—a move which in certain quarters would not be contemplated! Nevertheless, in that first year every athlete in the championships recorded personal bests. Main attraction at the 1985 title-decider was the new 1500 metres championship record by Alastair Walker at 4 mins. 5.4 secs., beating Ian Elliot's 4:17.3 set in 1970. (Ian actually holds the club record for the 1500 metres and mile, though at the time he was a member of Edinburgh Southern and only second-claim Teviotdale. At Hawick in 1975, he clocked 4 mins. 4 secs. for the 1500 metres and that same year when competing at Gateshead for the city club returned a mile time of 4:5.4, a 3:47 1500 metres). Other highlights since moving to Tweedbank have come from Michael Bryson who picked up four titles in 1986 (youths 100 metres, 1500 metres, long jump and javelin); Keith Logan who produced a notable "double" with the one-lap sprint and metric mile titles in 1987; and Judith Murray, in the same year, who won the 100 metres and 800 metres championships.

The official opening of the Tweedbank track was marked by the Celtic Games and Teviotdale's Angela McClure was in an invitation event between the "B" runners of the participating countries which were Scotland, Wales, Northern Ireland and Eire. Angela was fourth in the ladies' 100 metres in a personal best of 13.4 secs.

Too numerous to give full coverage to are the many runners who have turned out for Teviotdale in both club and open events be it track or cross-country. International standard may not have been reached but they are every bit as important to the strength of the club. Joanne McLeod, Diane Yellowlees, Lynn and Jane Hogg, Michael Bryson, Lynn Martin, Sandie Spence, Donald Hughes, Martin Bailey, Adam Bell and Adrian Murphy have won Border Championships. Karen Wear, Kirsty Mackintosh, Steven Rae, Adrian Spence, Bill Knox, Julie Scott, Norman Taylor, Alan Clyne, Alan Carruthers, Andy Fair, Keith Elliot and Brian Law have won club trophies.

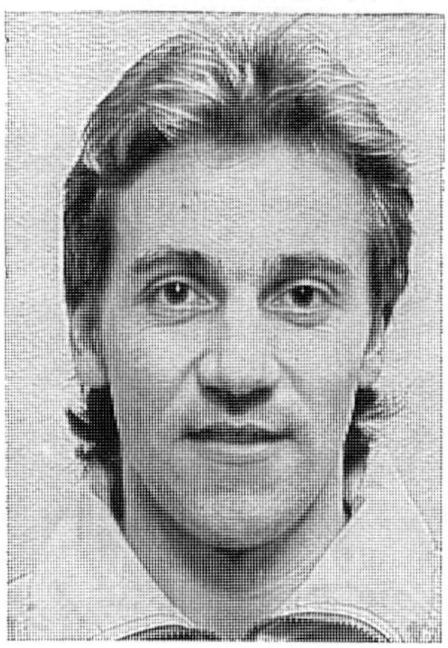

Colin Hume who represented Scotland in the 3000 metres steeplechase in the 1986 Commonwealth Games in Edinburgh. Colin was a prominent Teviotdale Harrier before joining Edinburgh Southern.

Colette Livingston, first winner of the Fire Brigade Cup in 1985, receives the trophy from Sub-Officer R. Wishart, on behalf of his Fire Service colleagues who raised the money for the award. Colette was the daughter of a local fireman!

Prizewinners in the 1982 Burns Club races with Burns Club officials R. Marshall, president (seated centre) and H. Mitchell, treasurer (top right).

THE "FUN DAYS"

No history of Teviotdale Harriers would be complete without mentioning the "fun days." On these occasions the object is to enjoy an afternoon in the company of fellow members and indulge in some form of competition but still with the thought that "its all in a day's fun" uppermost in everyone's mind.

Such a day is the Christmas relay, popularly referred to at one time as the "Curny Banna Stakes." The name was derived from the prizes won. Every competitor receives a festive season prize of Christmas cakes, currant buns or shortbread, etc., and the better a team is placed the greater the reward. But it is all one big "fun day."

The origins of an event at this time of year could be a race first run in 1910 between the captain's team and the vice-captain's team. In 1928 it was changed to a 10-mile team relay.

The first mention of a Christmas relay in Wilton Lodge Park was in the minutes of a committee meeting held in October 1948. It was decided to hold a team relay race on Christmas day and that all runners receive a prize. Entry was to be 6d (2½p) per man. The course was to start at the Museum then up to the Dunk, round past the tennis courts, across Langlands Bridge, down through the Playing Fields, across the Laurie Bridge and back to the Museum. This course of 2¼-miles is still used to this day. If any times were taken these were to be unofficial and not for the benefit of the handicapper.

The inaugural relay race was voted a great success by all who took part. The runners were split into five teams of four. The teams were fairly evenly matched and it was much to the credit of the handicapper that only 200 yards separated the first and last runner. At the first change-over the "A" team led but by the next stage the "D" team had taken over. In the third stage, the "B" team moved into second place behind "D". Then in the final circuit, Benny Murray pulled back the "D" team's lead to give the "B" team victory. This report of the race was taken from the "Hawick Express," unfortunately the team members were not given. Neither the club's Minute Book nor the "Hawick News" files contain details of the historic occasion. There is, however, details available of the 1949 event. This was won by a team captained by Douglas Campbell and comprising W. Duncan, A. Arres and D. Murray. Douglas also captained the winning team the following year.

Given below are some statistics from over the years:—

1955—Winning team: R. Wilkinson, D. Oliver, M. Shankie, G. Moyes.

1960—Winning team: B. Mather, D. Campbell, W. Riddell, D. Roebuck.

1962—Winning team: G. Shiel, D. Jeffrey, P. Turnbull, C. Douglas. Winning ladies' team: J. Green, E. Petrie, A. Fox.

1968—Turnout of 48 competitors.

1971—From an entry of over 60 the winning team was S. Lunn, W. Lindsay, D. Henderson, A. Fox.

1973—Such was the entry, three separate relays were run.

1975—Entry of 66 runners.

1976—Turnout of 80 competitors.

1982—With Wilton Lodge Park being partly flooded due to recent heavy rain, the relay race was over a new course. The winning team was M. Borthwick, D. Yellowlees, C. Pringle, G. McCusker, C. Hamilton, N. Hall.

1985—Fourteen teams of six contested the relay — the biggest ever turnout — with the winning team comprising A. Murphy, L. Hogg, J. Graham, C. Pringle, B. Law, A. Casson.

1987—Winning team: C. Nichol, A. Reid, B. Gibb, J. Anderson, A. Murphy, B. Gibson.

Another form of "fun day" were the outings to St Mary's Loch, organised by club members Willie Lindsay and George Meikle. The outing in December 1974 comprised an 8-mile race round the loch, won by I. Elliot; guessing tree variety—D. McGinn; guessing time of race—S. Lunn; and mystery place in race—G. Scott. Retiring to the Gordon Arms for tea and further merriment, the domino tournament was won by J. Bouglas and the darts by A. Samuel.

Occasionally there have been fishing competitions, club member Arthur Oliver donating a trophy. In July 1979 the venue was Hellmoor Loch when 200 perch and three trout were taken. The winner of the trophy (heaviest catch) was J. Bouglas, with other prizes going to C. McLeod, first junior; J. Rudkin, first guest; C. McLeod, biggest fish ($1\frac{1}{4}$-lb. trout); and Shona Cumming, the only girl, won the "booby" with three perch.

Hellmoor Loch was also the venue in July 1982 when D. Rudkin won the Arthur Oliver Trophy with a 3-lb. catch which included a 2-lb. trout.

An event which has now been established as a firm favourite is the Ne'er Day run. On the first day of 1987, for example, 30 runners turned out for a most enjoyable outing.

Former Cup race winners who were guests at Hawick Moor in March 1984. They are (left to right)—W. Smith (Junior, 1933-34); G. Lumsden (1934); A. Kyle (1930); G. Turnbull (1939, 1949, 1951); and V. Law (1959).

Prizewinners in the 1986 Burns Club races. The trophies and medals were presented by Bert Duncan (centre), Burns Club vice-president.

BOYS' SECTION FROM 1980

In the 1980-81 cross-country season, the Eastern District unofficial colts' league was dominated by Teviotdale's Chris Murphy — he won all three — and with clubmates Michael Bryson and Graeme Robertson, Teviotdale was runner-up in the team placings for the season. The Eastern District Championships of 1981 also saw Teviotdale colts finish second, the team being Murphy, Bryson and Kevin Turnbull. Murphy won the race and he did so the following year but it is an unofficial championship at that level and no title is given. The 1981-82 cross-country league programme was also "Murphy's season." He won the second race and was runner-up in the third. In the Scottish Championships that season the junior boys (19, George McCusker; 31, Graeme Pringle; 35, David Rudkin; 48, Scott Brannan) were sixth from 22 clubs, the best team placing for 10 years.

Back to the cross-country league and in the first race (October) in the 1982-83 season, Teviotdale's young athletes had one of their most successful days. Colin Nichol was first senior boy; Daren Thomson second colt; and George McCusker and Chris Murphy finished second and third respectively in the junior boys. That same month the Scottish Relay Championships were hosted by the Hawick club — the first time they had been held in the Borders — and with the administration and presentation of prizes being held at the Teviotdale Leisure Centre, the complex received its best publicity since opening. The event itself was staged a couple of miles away at the racecourse at Hawick Moor and from 600 competitors, the young athletes were the best from the host club, placed seventh. The second league race in November 1982 saw the junior boys come from third to the top of the table with: 1, Murphy; 5, McCusker; 18, Robertson. Colin Nichol was second in the senior boys. The following month Teviotdale had five runners in the East team for the inter-district match against the North and West, junior boys Chris Murphy and George McCusker finishing second and 10th respectively; senior boy Colin Nichol was third, the first East runner; and youths Alan Clyne and Ronnie Nichol were 14th and 19th respectively.

In the first month of 1983 T.H.C. had yet another of their highly successful days in open competition when the junior boys crushed the opposition to win the Eastern District Championship and club runners also lifted two individual titles. The team championship came from: 1, George McCusker; 2, Chris Murphy; 6, Graeme Robertson — the runners-up well back on 24 points! Adding to McCusker's individual title, Colin Nichol completely dominated the senior boys' championship, winning by 100 yards. In 1984 McCusker had to move up to senior boy level but nevertheless was an easy winner of the Eastern District title. With form such as that it came as no surprise two weeks later when the junior boys won the third and final league race and the league outright by six points from the mighty Edinburgh Southern. The boys brought the Teribus Trophy back to Hawick for the fourth time since it was presented to the Eastern District by Teviotdale in 1967. The team placings were: 1, McCusker; 4, Murphy; 6, Robertson. Nichol again won the senior boys' league race. The following month (February 1983), the junior boys were in top form again, this time in the Scottish Championships where they finished runners-up with: 7, Murphy; 10, McCusker; 35, Robertson; 61, Derrick Riddell. A medal for young Riddell brought back similar memories for his father Dennis, competing in the senior event that day. The latter was a member of the T.H.C. junior team which finished third in 1960 and first in 1961. The junior boys were still to the fore in the 1983-84 league programme with Murphy recording two thirds and a second. The team finished the league runners-up, other counters during the season being Robertson, Chay Campbell and Daren Thomson. The senior boys that season came from eighth after the first race to second in the other two with counters such as McCusker, Brian Law and David Rudkin.

David Rudkin (left) and Graeme Pringle, winners of the boys' handicap at the Hawick R.F.C. Sevens in 1983 and 1984 respectively.

Eastern District Junior Boys' Champions, 1983—(left to right)—Graeme Robertson, George McCusker and Chris Murphy. McCusker was also the individual champion.

The Teviotdale team who were runners-up in 1983 in the Scottish Junior Boys' Cross-Country Championship. They are (left to right)—Chris Murphy, Derrick Riddell, George McCusker and Graeme Robertson.

DISTRICT RELAY CHAMPIONS

"Gold" came to Teviotdale in October 1983 when the young athletes (junior boy, senior boy and youth) won the Eastern District Relay Championship from 43 teams. In fact the 'B' string came 10th that day and all that against such clubs as Edinburgh Southern, Edinburgh A.C. and Aberdeen who each fielded 10 teams. The T.H.C. trio was Murphy (2nd), Rudkin (2nd) and Nichol (1st). Fielding the same team the following week, the boys were runners-up to Ayr Seaforth in the National Relay Championship from 90 teams. In October 1984, once again T.H.C. young athletes were among the medals in the District Relay Championship on this occasion taking bronze. The team members were: 8, Steven Rae (junior boy); 5, Chris Murphy (senior boy); 3, Colin Nichol (youth).

Other notable performances from boys in the club came from George McCusker in smashing the M. and M. Trophy record by 13 secs. to 6 mins 1 sec. in 1983 and Donald Hughes, a colt showing great potential. He won the first league race in October 1986; the Berwick Walls race in September 1987 and within two days of that victory was the first holder of the Refuge Assurance Trophy.

Eastern District Young Athletes Relay Champions 1983—Chris Murphy (junior boy), David Rudkin (senior boy) and Colin Nichol (youth).

CHRIS MURPHY—A WORTHY SCOTTISH CHAMPION

Chris Murphy was showing all the qualities of being Teviotdale's brightest young star and this was sealed in February 1984 when he won the Scottish Cross-Country Championship—the Hawick club's first male athlete to do so. The 13-year-old swept all opposition aside in the junior boys' event to win the Alex Nangle Trophy and an impressive gold medal with his 50-yard victory.

Further mention must be made of the performances of Chris. As well as the prominent part he played in Teviotdale's team successes, he wrote his name into the club record books. In 1981 he won the colts' championship in a new record time of 5 mins. 10 secs. (the previous best by A. Lauder had stood since 1973) only to reduce this to 4:58 the following year. Also in 1982, he set a new record of 6:14 in the M. and M. Trophy race which had been held by Colin Nichol at 6:22. The boys' club championship went to Chris in 1984 and once again the record tumbled, the 1983 time of 8:21 by McCusker being reduced to 7:56.

Scottish Junior Boys' Champion in 1984 was Chris Murphy, the first Teviotdale male athlete to win a national cross-country title.

Alan Samuel (left) and George Meikle negotiate a gate at Highchesters on the club championship course.

Scottish track and cross-country internationalist; Scottish 1500 metres champion 1987; and club champion Joan Anderson.

Scottish cross-country internationalist Judith Murray.

LADIES' SECTION FROM 1980

The lead given by young Joan Anderson and Judith Murray both of whom achieved internationalist status—was instrumental in raising the standard among their clubmates.

Referring to team successes first, in the 1982-83 cross-country season, the minor girls finished a creditable fifth in the Scottish Road-Relay Championship with Sandra Lee, Linda Wilson, Sandra Gordon and Joan Anderson. In the open races at Annan, minor girls Joan Anderson, Sandra Gordon, Linda Wilson and Tracy Martin, lifted the team prize. Success had been kindled.

The Women's Eastern District Championships in 1985 produced a real heroine in 11-year-old Sandra Purdie, who won the minor girls. That day Joan Anderson was third in the girls' event and so was the team and third was also picked up by the intermediate team when their first counter Judith Murray was fourth. A few weeks later that trio was selected for the inter-district match in which Judith was fifth and both Sandra and Joan were second in their respective age groups. Successes in the 1985-86 cross-country season included Joan Anderson's win in the Lasswade open races plus the girls' team prize with Lynne Hogg and Sally Wight and the girls' bronze medal placing in the Scottish Championships with: 7, Joan Anderson; 26, Lynne Hogg; 28, Sally Wight; 59, Adrian Murphy. In November 1986 the Women's Eastern District Championships were held at Aberdeen and of the 10 Teviotdale girls who undertook the long journey North their performances were such that eight were selected for the East in the annual match against the West. At the championships, Joan Anderson won the junior title and Lynne Hogg was ninth; Judith Murray finished sixth in the intermediate; in the minor girls' race Melisa Traynor was third, Julie Scott sixth and Sandie Spence, ninth; and Sandra Purdie and Adrian Murphy were third and eighth respectively in the girls' event. All these girls represented the East. The best placings in the match came from Joan Anderson who picked up two awards, third overall and a counter in the winning East team and little Julie Scott, an outstanding sixth in the minor girls.

Cross-country club records in the John Elliot Trophy went to Sheila Douglas in 1981 (4 mins. 52 secs.) and Sandra Purdie (4:21) in 1987.

CLUB, DISTRICT AND SCOTTISH CHAMPION JOAN ANDERSON

The preceding pages have shown Joan Anderson to be one of Teviotdale's most outstanding athletes. From her early successes as a minor girl, she moved through the age groups and in open competitions her dedication set her above all her clubmates, be it on the track or cross-country. Joan was coached by her father, Adam, and a successful partnership it proved to be. In fact, Joan was instrumental in him joining the Harriers and in 1984 he won the Glencairn Trophy as the first veteran in the Cup race.

Like several Harriers before her, Joan rewrote the club's record book. Her record-breaking, club champion career started in 1982 when she took the minor girls' title in a new record time. For that she was tagged "the find of the season" and how true a comment that turned out to be. In 1985 she clocked the best time of 7 mins. 40 secs. in the Fire Brigade Cup, only to take another 12 secs. off it the following year; also in 1985 she won the Douglas Trophy for the girls' championship, cutting the record by 13 secs; and the record in the John Elliot Trophy race in 1984 went to Joan at 4 mins. 36 secs., beating the previous best by 16 secs. and then again in 1985 at 4.23. Further club records fell to her in 1987—the Ladies' Challenge Trophy in 6 mins. 31 secs., that was by 38 secs. from Pauline Cairns' time which had stood for seven years; she took 25 secs. off the Ladies' Jubilee Trophy; and equalled the record in the senior ladies' club championship in her first season at that level.

In open competition, as well as figuring in the club's team success, Joan had a string of individual successes to her credit. As a minor girl, 1983 and 1984, she was runner-up in the Eastern District Championship. To get to the 1984 event at Cumbernauld, the car in which she was a passenger only managed to get back home by following a snow plough through the drifts on Soutra Hill—surely that is what one would call dedication and a quality she has shown ever since.

Her first cross-country "cap" or "vest" as it is correctly termed in athletics, came in 1984 when she represented Scotland in the inter-league match at Ipswich, finishing 43rd as the seventh Scottish counter. The following year she was in the Home Counties International at Leeds. In 1986 she again represented Scotland in the inter-league match, on this occasion at Nottingham, finishing seventh as third team counter. She won the 3000 metres Kodak Classic in Glasgow in March 1986—her prize, a camera, of course; and her win in the junior ladies' event at Livingston in the October that year, for which she was awarded the Ben McGill Memorial Trophy, heralded the start of a fantastic run of successes in the 1986-87 cross-country season. She won the open races at Bonnyrigg, Penicuik, Dunbar, Edinburgh and Grangemouth; and won one league race and was second in two others. Underlining her high standing in Scottish athletics and adding to the "gold" she won in the Eastern District Cross-Country Championships in November 1986, Joan finished in the bronze medal position in the Scottish Championships (junior ladies) in February 1987. She completed the season runner-up in the Kodak Classic in Glasgow.

Success has also come her way on the track, winning the junior ladies' 1500 metres in 5 mins. 10.2 secs. in the Eastern District Championships in May 1986 and then retaining her title the following year. She started the 1987 track season in the limelight by winning the 1500 metres at the opening of the new Carlisle stadium and that in 4 mins. 49 secs., a personal best by 16 secs. That was the second fastest by a Teviotdale girl, the best being the 4:41.6 recorded by Pauline Cairns during her heyday of 1979-81. At the Scottish Schools' Championships, Joan won her age group 1500 metres and that led to her running in the British Championships held at Tweedbank in which she finished seventh. The first Scot to finish, 14-year-old Joan was competing in the under-17 age group so her performance was commendable. It came as no surprise that year when Joan won the Scottish junior ladies' 1500 metres title. A "cap" in the Celtic Games in Antrim, the track international between Scotland, Wales, Northern Ireland and Eire, resulted in Joan winning the 1500 metres event in a personal best of 4 mins. 40 secs.—only one second slower than the winner of the older age group—a new best performance by a Teviotdale girl. In the spring of 1988, Joan left Teviotdale to join Edinburgh Southern Harriers.

CROSS-COUNTRY INTERNATIONALIST JUDITH MURRAY

In the shadow of Joan Anderson has been Teviotdale's other lady internationalist Judith Murray.

At intermediate level, she gained her first "cap" in the Home Countries International at Leeds in December 1985 and two weeks later ran for Scotland in the Five Nations International Championships at Alexandra Palace, London. In 1986 she was in a Scottish vest for the inter-league match at Nottingham, finishing as third team counter in the intermediate event. At club level her successes included the 1985-86 Ladies' Jubilee Trophy in a new record time. On the track Judith was third in the intermediate 800 metres in the 1986 Eastern District Championships.

"MARATHON MAN" AND "MOUNTAIN MAN"

Some club members are not content to adhere to the conventional event—they have to increase the challenge. Two such runners are Stuart Bennett and John Marsh.

The former tackles events that most runners would shy well clear of—anything up to 50 miles! In August 1981, Stuart was in the 36½-mile Two Bridges race (Kincardine Bridge and Forth Bridge) finishing 21st, the third Scot, in 3 hrs. 57 mins. 20 secs. At his fourth attempt, in 1984, he was 10th in 3:49:52, his best time by 8 mins. Another specialist event "Marathon Man" Stuart tackled was the 53½-mile London to Brighton road-race, that was in 1982. At that first attempt at a "double marathon" the 37-year-old clocked in at 7 hrs. 12 mins. for 48th place from 170 starters. Training for that type of event was not easy. For example, in 1983, Stuart covered 4700 miles, there being only eight days in the year when he was not either competing or training.

Stuart's greatest achievement was in 1984 when he set a new Scottish native and national record for the 24-hour track race at his first attempt. He covered 141 miles 1140 yards in the allotted time, the previous best being 136 miles 1390 yards. He received a medal as his reward, described by Stuart as a "survivors medal"—no one could dispute that!

The Ben Nevis race has attracted several Teviotdale runners over the years, none more so than John Marsh—he has made the 4400 feet ascent on 12 occasions with a best time to date of 1 hr. 42 mins. 39 secs. in 1983 and a best placing of 34th in 1987.

"Mountain Man" John is well known for his own particular tests of stamina and endurance. He has travelled great distances to take part such as the Bens of Jura race (16 miles and 7500 feet ascent); Ben Lomond race (9 miles and 3000 feet); Goatfell race, Isle of Arran; "Three Peaks" race, North Yorkshire (22 miles and 4000 feet); Horseshoe fell race (9 miles and 3000 feet); Two

Stuart Bennett

John Marsh

Breweries race from Traquair to Broughton (18 miles and 5000 feet); and the Arrochar Hill race which covers 13 miles taking in four peaks each with a 3000 feet ascent.

HARRIERS RISE TO NEW HEIGHTS

"The greatest experience of their lives" was how three members of Teviotdale Harriers described their successful attempt at the 24-hour "Three Peaks" race in July 1987. This entailed running to the top of the three highest peaks in Scotland, Wales and England—and all in the space of 24 hours. Those who faced the 900 miles travelling and some eight hours actual running time, were Stuart Bennett, Bill Knox and Andy Fair, with Neil Dalgetty as the driver. Stuart, of course, was not new to such feats, Bill had the experience of a few fell races but Andy was a novice where such endurance-testing events were concerned. They tackled Snowdon on a fine Friday at 8 p.m., that took two hours, followed by Scafell at 4 a.m. where they got lost for a spell due to the atrocious weather conditions and had to use a map and compass to find the summit. That took over three hours. For the ascent of Ben Nevis on the Saturday afternoon when they managed to persuade Neil to accompany them, they were blessed with fine weather. In all, the race—or would it not be better described as an assault course—took them 20 hours 45 minutes 16 seconds and they were none the worse for their experience.

That type of running brings to mind the exploits of Teviotdale Harrier Maxwell Telford. A frequent competitor in the Ben Nevis race and seventh in the 1962 Scottish marathon championship, he is better known for his tests of stamina and endurance while he was an "exile" in New Zealand. In 1964, he set the New Zealand 100-mile fastest time with 14 hrs. 58 mins.; he competed in a 700-mile event in 1967 and in 1969 ran the 100 miles round Mount Egmont in 16 hrs. 10 mins., breaking the previous record by 6 hrs. 35 mins.

The "Three Peaks" squad (left to right)—Bill Knox, Stuart Bennett, Neil Dalgetty (driver) and Andy Fair.

Colin Nichol, the 1983 Eastern District Senior Boys' Champion.

Alastair Walker, senior cross-country club champion 1984, 1985, 1986; club championship record holder; 1500 metres champion 1985, 1986 and record holder.

ALASTAIR WALKER—FROM LINDEN RUGBY PLAYER TO SCOTTISH TEAM

As can be seen by the club's 1986-87 achievements, Alastair Walker played a prominent part.

Joining the Harriers in the 1983-84 season after playing rugby for Hawick Linden, Alastair went straight into the limelight with the best placings in the league races and District Championship that season. In that first year in the Harriers he won the 5-mile Menzies Trophy, then went on to take the 7-mile club championship from three-times holder Brian Emmerson. Though not reaching full international status, Alastair has competed twice for the Scottish Cross-Country Union in the match against Scottish Universities, Northern Ireland and Civil Service in 1984 and 1986, finishing 14th and 20th respectively. A cross-country club record went to him when he retained his senior title in 1985, breaking Martin Elsdon's 1979 time by 25 seconds, and on the track he set a new 1500 metres club championship record in 1985 of 4 mins. 5 secs., beating the 4:17.3 held by Ian Elliot since 1970. Alastair also has the distinction of the second best placing by a Teviotdale senior in the Scottish Cross-Country Championships. In 1985 he finished 17th. Only Craig Douglas at the height of his career bettered that by finishing 11th.

TEVIOTDALE HALF-MARATHON

The surge in the popularity of marathons and half-marathons on a national scale in the 1980s resulted in Teviotdale Harriers introducing the shorter distance event to the people of Hawick in July 1985.

In that first year there was an entry of over 300 and the townspeople turned out in their thousands to see this unique spectacle. Sponsorship for the event came from several local firms, the principal being the Martin Elsdon Sports Shop and in 1986, when almost 300 athletes took part, that main sponsor again came forward with prizes. That year also saw the introduction of a 2-mile fun run which attracted an entry of 200. For 1987, three Teviotdales joined in partnership. Teviotdale Design, the Hawick-based ceramic figures company, donated two perpetual trophies for the Third Teviotdale People's Half-marathon — one for the winner and the other for the first lady. Teviotdale Leisure Centre offered their facilities for the administration and presentation of prizes. But even more sponsorship was to come. In their national campaign "Make People Matter," N.A.L.G.O., the Local Government Officers' Union, came forward with a substantial contribution and with donations once again from several local firms, the day was once more a great success. On that occasion competitors in the fun run far outnumbered those in the "half," some 260 turning out to run 2 miles and receive a medal for the effort. Teviotdale Design sponsored the Half-marathon in 1988.

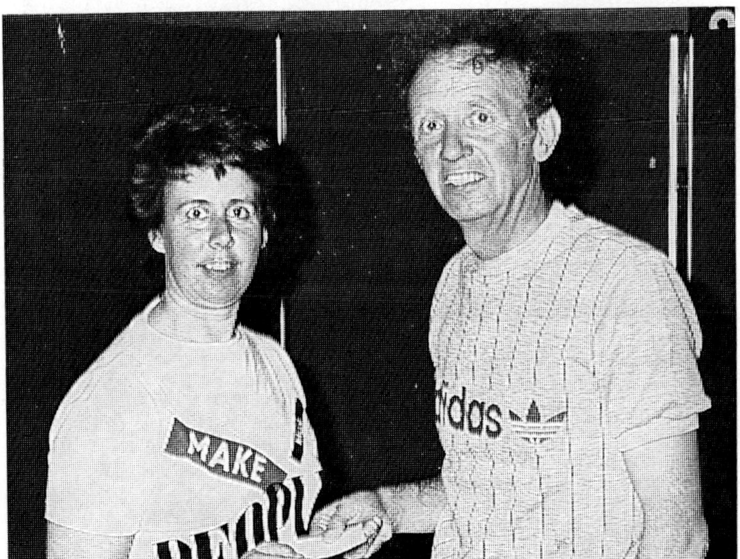

Diana Thomas, Borders branch secretary of N.A.L.G.O. (the union for local authority staff) hands over the sponsorship cheque for the 1987 Teviotdale half-marathon to race director Grant Moyes.

The scene in Hawick High Street in 1986 at the start of the second Teviotdale half-marathon.

They're off! The start of the 1986 fun run in Mansfield Road, held prior to the Teviotdale half-marathon.

Start of the fun run prior to the 1987 half-marathon.

Two Teviotdales joined forces in 1987 when new trophies were donated by Teviotdale Design, the Hawick-based ceramic figures company, for the winner and first lady in the Teviotdale half-marathon. In the picture are (left to right)—Maria Duggan (Teviotdale Design); Grant Moyes (Teviotdale Harriers race director); Deborah Edlmann and Derrick Moore (Teviotdale Design); and John Marsh (Teviotdale Harriers).

Teviotdale Harriers Dennis Riddell (no. 122) and Alex "Pecker" Renwick, stop for refreshment at the Hazeldean Lodge "watering station" in the 1987 Teviotdale half-marathon.

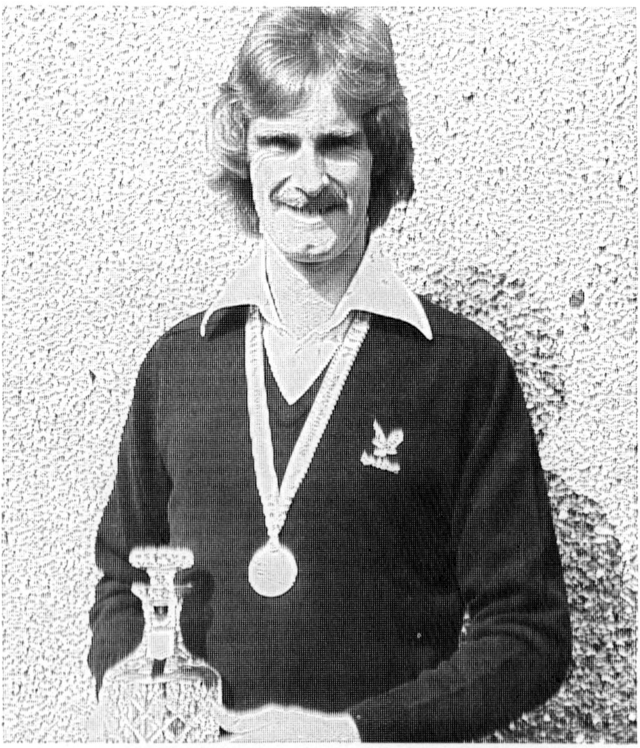

Ian Elliot—1970-71 captain; winner of the Senior Cup 1971; senior championship 1971; Jubilee Trophy 1976; Langheugh Trophy 1971, 1979, 1982, 1984; and Coltman Cup 1970. He is pictured here after finishing second in the 1983 Edinburgh Marathon.

Prominent Harriers of the 1980s, "snapped" as they completed the Teviotdale half-marathon. Brian Emmerson (above) and David Cavers

SENIORS OF THE 1980s EMULATE SUCCESSES OF 20 YEARS EARLIER

After 20 years in the sidelines of Scottish athletics, Teviotdale enjoyed a new found strength in depth at senior level and major successes quickly came their way.

The build-up to greater things started in the cross-country season of 1984-85 when the Hawick club made a "clean sweep" in the 10-mile Cockermouth road-race, finishing one, two and three with Brian Emmerson, Alastair Walker and Ian Elliot respectively and, of course, the team prize. Brian was a three-times club champion; Alastair the current title-holder; and Ian, back with his native club after a spell with Edinburgh Southern Harriers, had reached international status while an "exile." With a talent base like that and then runners such as David Cavers, Keith Elliot, Keith Logan, Andy Fair, Brian Neilson and Rob Hall joining them, the Hawick club was on its way up.

League race team placings of third and fourth in the 1985-86 season gave Teviotdale the much needed platform in which to launch an attack on the strong central Scotland clubs, which they did in the Eastern District Relay Championships for the McKenzie Trophy taking the bronze medal position—the best placing since 1966—with Cavers, Emmerson, K. Elliot and Walker. Such was their strength they were able to field teams who finished 24th, 25th and 39th from the 72 entered. With the same quartet, their sixth place from 138 teams in the 4 x 2½-mile McAndrew Relay at Glasgow, from a poor 34th in 1984, was highly commendable in that very competitive major relay. The 34th place was their worst ever yet 12 months later they produced their best since 1963. For the Scottish Relay Championships the same squad was called upon yet again and they finished sixth—at the time the best ever placing—and that from 120 teams. The National Six-stage Relay that season also resulted in Teviotdale having, at the time, their best ever placing, which was eighth from 105 teams, the previous best was 12th in 1984. The team was K. Elliot, Emmerson, Logan, Cavers, Fair and Walker. In 1987 the team was even better finishing fifth.

A SEASON OF ACHIEVEMENTS

The 1986-87 season will never be forgotten. "This was their finest hour" is a phrase that could have been used on several occasions as each time their achievement surpassed the previous one. The season's successes started with the McAndrew Relay in October in which Teviotdale finished fourth from 200 teams—the first East team. The team was Emmerson, Cavers, Hall and Walker. For the Eastern District Relay Championships, Edinburgh Southern pulled in four internationalists, including three Commonwealth Games athletes, to take the McKenzie Trophy, with the Hawick club putting in a commendable bid to lift the silver medals from 58 teams. The team and times were: Emmerson (12 mins.); Cavers (11.59); I. Elliot (12.00) and Walker (12.03)—a very evenly matched quartet. With strength in depth Teviotdale also fielded teams who finished 9th, 19th, 23rd, 32nd and 39th. Next came the National Cross-Country Relay Championship and Teviotdale's fifth place became their best ever. The team was Emmerson, Hall, Elliot and Walker. That same quartet then tackled the 4 x 5-mile Allan Scally Memorial Trophy road-race, one of the most keenly contested relays in the Scottish calendar with all the leading clubs competing. From over 120 teams, Teviotdale once again finished in the silver medal position.

INTER-CITY MERITORIOUS MEDALS

Twenty of the top clubs in Scotland receive an invitation to compete in the annual 44¼-mile Edinburgh to Glasgow road-relay and in 1986 Teviotdale was one of them. In 1981 — the last occasion in which they were invited — T.H.C. finished 18th but fortunes had changed dramatically since then and they finished ninth to once again be awarded the special medals as the "most meritorious unplaced team." The runners, individual placings and distances were: Ian Elliot (17th) 5½ miles; Brian Emmerson (17th) 6 miles; Brian Neilson (13th) 4½ miles; Keith Elliot (12th) 5½ miles; Alastair Walker (10th) 5¾ miles; Rob Hall (10th) 6½ miles; David Cavers (9th) 5½ miles; Andy Fair (9th) 5½ miles. Walker's time of 29 mins. 22 secs. was the fastest in that stage.

Teviotdale had never won the 9-mile Brampton to Carlisle road-race but that was rectified in November 1986 when the formidable Rob Hall, Brian Emmerson and Ian Elliot partnership were victors in what is considered one of the top team events in the North of England.

WORTHY LEAGUE CHAMPIONS

The seniors' 1986-87 Eastern District League programme was on a high note all season culminating in their first ever outright league win. Decided from three fixtures, it opened at Hawick in October with Teviotdale winning by 53 points from Edinburgh A.C. The Hawick club had six counters in the first 18 to finish, they were: 2, Emmerson; 3, Hall; 6, Cavers; 9, Walker; 17, Logan; 18, I. Elliot. Though going into the second league race at West Calder in December with a weakened team due to illness, T.H.C. still managed to finish runners-up to Falkirk and retained the top placing by 29 points. Best for Teviotdale was Emmerson, ninth, followed by: 12, Hall; 15, Cavers; 17, Neilson; 25, Logan and a commendable 32 from Rob Templeman. The "Maroons" took the field in the third and final race at Edinburgh in January with Falkirk having topped the league in the previous three years. Putting six counters into the first 21 finishers was enough to clinch the league title and with it the impressive George Sandilands Shield. The result was: Teviotdale, 43 points; Edinburgh A.C., 90; Falkirk, 147. The individual placings were: 2, Emmerson; 3, Walker; 4, Cavers; 6, I. Elliot; 7, Hall; 21, Logan. Such was the tremendous back-up, the next six Teviotdale seniors were seventh, a placing which would have been highly thought of from the "firsts" at one time. The six were: 31, Brian Neilson; 35, Keith Elliot; 38, Andy Fair; 47, Bill Knox; 69, Alan Clyne; 80, Rob Templeman. In the newly constituted overall league, comprising results from the five age groups, T.H.C. were runners-up to Edinburgh A.C., with Edinburgh Southern third.

The 1986-87 season "double".—winners of the Eastern District Senior Championship and League. Those involved in the historic "double" are (standing, left to right)—Ian Elliot, David Cavers, Keith Logan, Brian Emmerson, Keith Elliot, Ross Templeman and Rob Hall, and (seated) Alastair Walker (Ronnie Pringle, club president) and Brian Neilson.

A SEASON "DOUBLE"

The Hawick club's strength at senior level in 1986-87 was underlined when their first ever league and championship "double" was achieved. The T.H.C. heroes pulled off a massive 67-point victory to lift the Thomas Fraser Memorial Cup in the Eastern District Cross-Country Championship. Team placings were: Teviotdale, 104 points; 2, Aberdeen, 171; 3, Pitreavie, 201, and individual counters were: 4, Cavers; 10, Walker; 14, I. Elliot; 15, Emmerson; 25, Hall; 36, Neilson. The title came against competition from 30 clubs and individual placings from a field of over 400. Teviotdale successes did not stop with the seniors that day. In the junior men's championship Colin Nichol picked up a bronze medal.

Thought to be the oldest Harrier ever to win the Senior Cup is 48-year-old Grant Moyes in 1987.

Father and son's Cup "double". The Duff family, in their first season in the Harriers, were successful in the 1985 Cup races at Hawick Moor racecourse. Thirty-eight-year-old Robert won the senior event and 15-year-old Robert (left) won the junior race with twin brother Ronald third.

Seniors in the 1987-88 opening run. Captain Alex "Pecker" Renwick is on president Ronnie Pringle's right.

Colts, junior boys, senior boys and youths in the 1987-88 opening run. Junior captain Colin Pringle is on president Ronnie Pringle's right.

Minor girls, girls and ladies in the 1987-88 opening run. Ladies' captain Joan Anderson is on president Ronnie Pringle's left.

Brian Neilson shows fellow Harriers how to tackle a gate. The incident is in the 1987-88 season Jubilee Trophy race.

CLUB RACE HIGHLIGHTS

In the period currently under review, (1980-1988) there were many achievements at club level, some of which are now given:

1982—The Knox family's running tradition with Teviotdale was continued when Bill Knox won the Cup race, then older brother Jim won the Langheugh Trophy in 1983 and the following year Bill won the Jubilee Trophy, only to repeat it in 1987. Their father, Willie, won both the club championship and Jubilee Trophy in 1947.

1983—The Menzies Trophy race included 65-year-old Duncan Bett, probably the oldest competitor ever in a club race.

1984—Colin Hume smashed the eight-year-old Menzies Trophy record by 48 secs. He had just returned home from a three-year athletics scholarship at Memphis State University in America. Colin, a member of Teviotdale in his younger days, joined Edinburgh Southern and went on to international honours, including the Scottish steeplechase championship in 1985 and selection for the 1986 Commonwealth Games in Edinburgh.

1985—Robert Duff and son Robert, both in their first season with T.H.C., pulled off a unique "double" by winning the Senior Cup and Junior Cup and the family went one better with young Robert's twin brother Ronald who was third in the junior event. The Riddell family can claim a similar feat but not on the same day. The Senior Cup was won by Billy in 1964 and 1965—the only person ever to win in successive years—and younger brother Dennis in 1966. The latter's son, Derrick, won the Junior Cup in 1984. Dennis, also won the Glencairn Trophy as the first veteran to finish in the Senior Cup race in 1983 and 1987.

1986—The Langheugh Trophy was sponsored for the first time by Burnfoot butcher John Marsh, himself a Langheugh Trophy winner in 1972 and 1975 and still turning out in a Teviotdale vest. In the 1987 event, he was the sponsor again—also the handicapper (not his own mark one would hasten to add) and the winner! He went on to retain the trophy in 1988.

1987—The 7-mile cross-country club championship was a real "ding-dong" affair in which the title could have gone to any of six athletes. The field of 21 included four former champions and was the toughest contest since the dead-heat between Jim Jack and Rob Renton in 1958. Only 62 secs. separated the first six to finish with three-times champion Brian Emmerson getting the title back again after being runner-up for the previous three years.

Winner of the Senior Cup at the Moor was Grant Moyes, who, at 48 years of age, is thought to be the oldest Harrier ever to win the coveted trophy. Other "veteran" winners that come to mind are 38-year-old George Turnbull in 1951 and 45-year-old Willie Lindsay in 1974.

Prizewinners in the Burns Club races run in December 1987. Trey are (left to right): back row—Steven Rae, Burns Club Trophy; Bert Duncan, Burns Club president; Ronnie Pringle, Teviotdale president; Keith Logan, Will Clark Memorial Trophy. Front row—Adrian Murphy (ladies); Bruce Hughes (colts); and Melissa Traynor (girls).

Steven Anderson sprinting to the finishing line to win the colts' event on Menzies Trophy race day, December 1987.

Joe Darcy, winner of the Jubilee Trophy in the 1987-88 season.

Scott Watson winning the colts' event on Langheugh Trophy race day, January, 1988.

Flying the flag. Steven Rae winning the Burns Club Trophy in December 1987 for the second time.

Youngsters start the first leg of the 1987 Christmas Relay in Wilton Lodge Park.

A changeover in the 1987 Christmas Relay in Wilton Lodge Park. The runners are (left to right) — Stuart Bennett, Derek Clyne, Robert Duff, John Marsh and Ian Murdie.

Colin Murray (no. 146), Gavin McAuley (no. 147) and Gary Froud (no. 61) battle for the minor placings in the colts' race on Jubilee Trophy race day, October, 1987.

Melissa Traynor winning the minor girls'/girls' event on Burns Club Trophy race day, December 1987.

Bruce Hughes winning the colts' event on Jubilee Trophy race day, October 1987. He also won the club colts' race the following month.

Ready, steady, go! Pauline Yule, the youngest competitor in the club races in December 1987.

Janey Hewat winning the Ladies' Jubilee Trophy in October 1987.

Junior captain Colin Pringle on his way to winning the Lodge 424 Trophy in October 1987.

The leading pack in the senior race in the Eastern District Cross-Country Championships staged at Hawick in January, 1988. David Cavers (no. 29) and Alastair Walker (no. 60) are the main Teviotdale challengers at this stage. Northern Ireland steeple-chaser Peter McColgan (no. 356), husband of Scotland's Liz Lynch, was the winner of the individual title.

Included in this group of Teviotdale seniors in the 1938 Eastern District Cross-Country Championships held at Hawick are: (left to right)—Alastair Walker, Brian Neilson, Rob Hall, David Cavers, Francis Cannon, Keith Logan, Colin Nichol, Alan Clyne, John Marsh, Joe Darcy and Bill Knox.

Rob Hall (no. 38) the first senior team counter when Teviotdale Harriers won the Eastern District Cross-Country Championship staged at Hawick in January, 1988. Behind Hall is team-mate Brian Emmerson (no. 36).

It was "mud, mud, glorious mud" and follow the leader for Teviotdale seniors Alan Reid (no. 51) and Jim Knox (no. 40) in Overhall Plantation during the 1988 Eastern District Championships at Hawick.

Feet disappear in the mud as Keith Logan (no. 43) and Keith Elliot (no. 35) of Teviotdale Harriers tackle the route through Overhall Plantation in the Eastern District Championships at Hawick in January, 1988.

SENIORS' ACHIEVEMENTS CONTINUE

Teviotdale's 1987-88 cross-country programme started where they left off the previous season—dominating the Eastern District and keeping among the leading clubs in Scotland.

In September, their formidable relay squad of Ian Elliot, Brian Emmerson, Alastair Walker and Rob Hall went straight into the new season runners-up to Sunderland in the 4 x 3-mile Presto road-race at Gateshead and the following week T.H.C. showed that they were going to be a force to be reckoned with in the major competitions when they lifted the team award in the

Brian Wear of Teviotdale tries to avoid the worst of the mud in the senior boys' race when the 1988 Eastern District Championships were staged at Hawick.

Flying high—Scott Amos (left) successfully makes it to the other side in the 1988 Langheugh Trophy race. Also negotiating the barbed wire and dyke at Whitehaugh Moor is Alan Reid (right), and Andrew Shankie (centre) sees what he has yet to tackle.

"Running of the Walls" races at Berwick. On that occasion the team was:— 2, David Cavers; 10, Andy Fair; 17, Brian Neilson.

Another great morale-booster was their second place in the prestigious McAndrew Relay at Glasgow from 152 teams. The team counters were—Emmerson, Cavers, Hall and Walker, and the 'B' string comprising Ian Elliot, Andy Fair, Brian Neilson and Keith Logan were 12th—a placing which in the past would have been commendable by the Hawick "firsts." The 'A' team's placing in that 4 x $2\frac{1}{2}$-mile, highly competitive relay, which incidentally was the best by an East club, provided Teviotdale with the launch pad for a crack at the East of Scotland Cross-Country Relay Championship—a title which had eluded them since they won it in the three successive years from 1961. Being runners-up in 1986 and third in 1985, it was felt that the opportunity would never be better. But it was not to be. Once again Edinburgh Southern brought in their "big guns" and, fielding four internationalists, pushed Teviotdale into the silver medal position for the second successive year. Teviotdale led for the first three stages with Emmerson, Cavers and Hall and it was the city club's onslaught in the final leg that overtook Walker. Teviotdale's 'B' squad, Ian Elliot, Andy Fair, Bill Knox and Keith Logan, finished a commendable fifth from the 87 teams entered.

Silver Medals Again

Two weeks later, the same 'A' squad forsook participation in the club's Jubilee Trophy race to compete in the tough Allan Scally Memorial Trophy road-race in Glasgow and once again they lifted silver medals. In a repeat of the District Relay Championships, Teviotdale were in the lead only to be overtaken in the final leg of the 4 x 5-mile event by Edinburgh Southern. This is considered one of the most keenly contested relays in Scotland and that day over 120 teams took part.

Next in the season's programme came the Scottish Relay Championships, hosted by Gala Harriers, and by all accounts they handled the administration admirably. The regular squad finished sixth, second East team, from the 150 entered, while the 'B' quartet were 18th.

A Disappointing Inter-City Run

Though finishing over 11 minutes faster than their 1986 time, T.H.C. could only manage eighth place in the Edinburgh to Glasgow road-relay race. This came as a bit of a disappointment to the team as they had set their sights on third place. However, eighth from the top 21 clubs in Scotland in this prestigious relay was one better than 1986 and after all it was their second best placing ever in the event. It will be recalled from a previous chapter, 1959 was the vintage year they finished sixth. The 1987 team members were:— Stage 1: B. Emmerson (2nd) 5½ miles; Stage 2: A. Walker (3rd) 6 miles; Stage 3: K. Logan (5th) 4½ miles (with the second fastest time for that stage); Stage 4: A. Fair (6th) 5½ miles; Stage 5: D. Cavers (5th) 5¾ miles; Stage 6: R. Hall (6th) 6½ miles; Stage 7: I. Elliot (6th) 5½ miles; Stage 8: B. Neilson (8th) 5½ miles.

Another disappointment during the 1987-88 season was not retaining the team trophy in the 10-mile Brampton to Carlisle road-race despite finishing first equal with Border Harriers. From a field of 700 the Teviotdale runners finished 5th (Walker); 7th (Emmerson) and 12th (Hall), while the English club were 6th, 8th and 10th. As Border's third runner was better than Teviotdale's, the trophy went to England. Walker led for the first seven miles and finished less than a minute behind the winner—the great Steve Cram. Teviotdale's 'B' team of Bill Knox, Andy Fair and Colin Nichol did well to finish eighth.

DISTRICT CHAMPIONSHIP RETAINED

The Eastern District Cross-Country Championships were staged at Hawick in January 1988 as a prelude to the National Championships which were coming to the town in February, 1989 in honour of Teviotdale's centenary. In a repeat of the previous season's championships, the Hawick club showed the 23 visiting teams that they reigned supreme in the District. Taking the field not only as defending champions but, at that time in the season, also league leaders, they kept the Thomas Fraser Memorial Cup in Hawick for another year, though by a much smaller margin than in 1987. The previous year they won by 67 points, in 1988 this was cut to 10, winning by 115 points to Aberdeen's 125, with Dundee on 157. All five events started and finished in Wilton Lodge Park but in between the runners were faced with mud which in places made feet disappear. Such were the underfoot conditions, following weeks of heavy rain, seven shoes were recovered from the mud at Overhall Farm after only three events. Teviotdale's victorious senior team counters were:— 8, Rob Hall; 9, David Cavers; 12, Alastair Walker; 13, Brian Emmerson; 28, Keith Logan; 45, Brian Neilson.

On facing page: (top) David Cavers leads the Teviotdale defence of the 1987-88 District League in the final match at Riccarton, Edinburgh. Bottom: Rob Hall and Alastair Walker (both no. 4) keeping up the pressure in the woodland section.

ANOTHER DISTRICT LEAGUE WIN

In October 1988, Teviotdale seniors commenced the defence of their Eastern District Cross-Country League title and it was a case of continuing where they left off the previous season—at the top of the table. The opening fixture was at Alloa which Teviotdale won by 61 points from Aberdeen A.C., with Edinburgh A.C., third. Spearheading the Hawick attack was David Cavers who won the 5-mile race, and with this tremendous performance in their sights, his team-mates were spurred on to pack all six counters into the first 19 runners from a field of over 200. After Cavers came: 6, Hall; 9, Walker; 10, Emmerson; 16, Logan; 19, Fair. In November, Teviotdale took a step nearer retaining their league title when the second race was staged at West Calder but before the day's results were formulated it had been a testing time for the Hawick club. With three of their top athletes, Hall, Elliot and Fair, absent through illness, T.H.C. were faced with a daunting task to hold their top-of-the-league place but they managed to do just that even though they only finished second on the day. Once again David Cavers was the team hero, winning his second successive league race. This fine performance was again instrumental in bringing out the best from Walker (3rd); Emmerson (6th); Logan (11th); Neilson (32nd) and Brian Law (61st). It was Neilson and Law, usually second string counters, who saved the day for Teviotdale, especially the latter who pulled back nine places in the closing stages. This tremendous team effort gave T.H.C. 114 points, only five behind Edinburgh A.C. Despite this second place, Teviotdale increased their lead in the table and went into the third and final league race with a massive 77-point advantage over the Edinburgh club. In the deciding fixture at Riccarton, Edinburgh, in February, 1988, Teviotdale were once again under pressure when Logan, Fair and Neilson were forced to call off through injury. For the second time reserves were called upon and they saved the day. Though finishing runners-up, to Aberdeen A.C. by 28 points that day, the Hawick club came out on top of the season's league programme by a margin of 51 points. The overall points tally was:— Teviotdale, 284; Aberdeen, 335; Edinburgh A.C., 423. Once again first to count for Teviotdale was David Cavers who was aiming for a league "hat-trick" but out of the pack came a Welsh internationalist running for Aberdeen. The northern city's representative was in the lead by 300 yards at one

---

On facing page: (top) Brian Emmerson, with Alastair Walker on the left, packing well in the league race at Riccarton. Bottom: On behalf of the league-winning Teviotdale team, David Cavers accepts the impressive George Sandilands Shield from Scottish Cross-Country Union president Fred McCluskie.

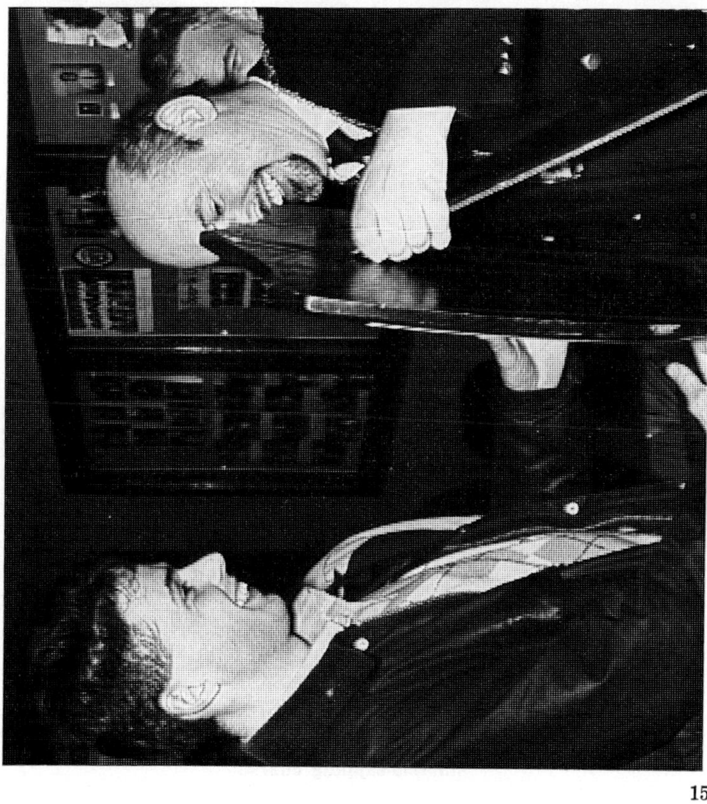

point but at the finish David had cut that to some 25 yards and could have won had the race been a little farther. Teviotdale's next three counters, Hall, Emmerson and Walker, were never out of the top 10, so much so, with some superb packing, they came home sixth, seventh and eighth respectively, with team-mates Bill Knox (38th) and Alan Clyne (48th) completing the counters for 109 points. For Knox and Clyne that was the first time they had counted for league points. Nevertheless, on the day, Aberdeen packed even better for 81 points but that was not enough to topple Teviotdale and so, after bringing the impressive George Sandilands Shield in the bus to Riccarton, it went straight back in triumph to reside in Hawick for another year.

In the youths' event was Chris Murphy, Teviotdale's former Scottish champion (see page 111). To the delight of the club supporters, Chris was in the leading pack right from the start and it was obvious that he would figure in the top placings. True enough, Chris took third place.

Getting back to top form, Chris Murphy (left) takes third place in the youths' event in the final Eastern District League race at Riccarton in February, 1988. Michael Bryson, also in the youths' event, finding it a stamina-sapping course.

The Eastern District includes the Edinburgh clubs as well as those from Falkirk, Dundee and Aberdeen, so in retaining the League as well as the Championship that season was the icing on the cake for Teviotdale seniors. In fact they had achieved what few clubs had ever done—won the two top District honours in successive years. It was significant that in the run-up to their centenary year, the club should emerge as true senior champions of the Eastern District.

NATIONAL AND DISTRICT RECOGNITION

Such was the top form of the runners in the white and maroon vests in the 1987-88 season, eight of them caught the eye of the National and District selectors. For the match at St Andrews in December 1987 between the Scottish Cross-Country Union, Scottish Universities, Northern Ireland and Civil Service, Brian

Donald Hughes who won the junior boys' cross-country championship in 1988.

Adrian Spence winning the John Elliot Trophy at Hawick Moor in March 1988 for the second successive year.

Emmerson ran for the S.C.C.U. team. Also at St Andrews that day, David Cavers, Alastair Walker and Keith Logan were included in the East team for the inter-District match against the West and North. Also representing the East in that match were Donald Hughes and Michael Bryson in the junior boys' and youth's events respectively.

Turning to the ladies' section, four of them were chosen to represent the East in their match against the West in December and from that performance two gained even higher honours. In the annual match, Joan Anderson (junior lady) finished third, Sandra Purdie (girl) was fifth and Julie Scott and Sandie Spence (minor girls) were ninth and 13th respectively. Joan and Sandra gained national recognition when both were included in the Scottish team for the inter-League match in London in January 1988. In this kind of mini British Championships, Joan, running for the fourth time in that match, finished second Scottish counter and 20th overall. Sandra finished eighth for Scotland and 41st overall.

Sporting a centenary T-shirt is Sandra Purdie who retained the Douglas Trophy in the 1988 girls' cross-country championship.

The 1987-88 cross-country season was certainly one in which the seniors stole the limelight and the only team successes from Teviotdale's younger age groups came from the minor girls and youths and both of those were in the club's open races in November 1987. The minor girls (3, Julie Scott; 6, Sandie Spence; 7, Kay Stenhouse—16 points) won the Stan Reid Memorial Trophy from Bo'ness, 36 points. The Army Careers Shield went to the youths when T.H.C. had 31 points to the 36 of Harmeny. The team counters were:— 6, Chris Murphy; 9, Michael Bryson; 16, Steven Rae.

The highest praise must go to the Teviotdale girls who made a round trip of almost 400 miles to compete in the Women's Eastern District Cross-Country Championships at Aberdeen in November 1987. Despite the tiring journey, Sandra Purdie lifted a silver medal in the girls' event—a performance which was instrumental in her Scottish "vest" for the inter-league match.

The expression says it all — it's been a hard race — but after six miles, John Marsh still has enough reserves to sprint to the finish of the 1988 Langheugh Trophy race and his second successive win.

A winning style — Adrienne Murphy on her way to lifting the Lodge 111 Trophy for ladies in January, 1988. In July 1988, she won a bronze medal in the Scottish junior 1500 metres championships.

Every one a trier. Competitors in the colts' cross-country championship in 1988 make a dash for the lead. The winner was Marc Wight (no. 8) second right.

Over the years many Harriers feet have pounded over this bridge at Woodfoot—once a well known Hawick landmark. The "Jooglie Brig," as it was known locally, was replaced in the 1970s. The new bridge features in several club courses including the senior championship and Menzies Trophy races.

AIRBORNE—Michael Bryson flying to the senior men's long jump title in the 1988 club championships at Tweedbank. The Teviotdale championships have been held at Tweedbank since it opened in 1984.

BATHTIME—About to get his feet wet at the water jump is Colin Nichol who won the 3000 metres steeplechase title at the 1988 club championships.

UP, UP AND AWAY—More like a dance routine than field events, Emma Milligan with the successful throw for the junior ladies' discus title in the 1988 club championships at Tweedbank.

A CHAMPION'S DETERMINATION— Kenneth Stewart attacks the bar in traditional style to win the junior boys' high jump title at the 1988 club championships at Tweedbank.

SUCCESSFUL FLOP—With a perfect "Fosbury Flop," Marc Wight wins the colts' high jump title in the 1988 club championships at Tweedbank.

REACHING FOR THE SKY—Junior captain Colin Pringle uses "The Flop" to set a new personal best during the 1988 club championships at Tweedbank.

THE NEXT 100 YEARS

And what of the future? Teviotdale Harriers have always been fortunate in having a strong body of administrative helpers, the vast majority of whom were active members in their younger days. Long may this situation continue, for no matter what the quality of its runners, a sound "behind-the-scenes" organisation is the foundation of a successful club.

In this modern world, attracting people of all ages and in particular youngsters, to active outdoor activities is a difficult task but the Harriers in Hawick are managing, though only through continued perseverence, to keep a strong club, comprising boys and girls from nine years and upwards, seniors and even veterans. With those turning out at the annual opening runs of the cross-country season now totalling almost 100 and club races attracting 60 to 80 competitors, the Harriers are the envy of many sporting clubs. The magnificent achievements from Teviotdale over the years have been a credit both to the club and the town and demonstrates the high level of commitment to the sport from both athletes and officials alike. Its participants and officials are the lifeblood of a club and without whose time, dedication, and enthusiasm Teviotdale Harriers, with its many honours, be they at local or national level, would not be the club it is today.

This history of one of Hawick's foremost sporting clubs is concluded with comments from guest speakers at two annual dinners. Though both have already been mentioned in an earlier chapter, their message is even more relevant on the club reaching its centenary. In 1935, John Purdom, who had been the first captain, said: "The club was formed with the idea of providing clean honest, healthy sport. It has justified its existence and has carried out the spirit in which it was born." At the 1948 function, Bob Crawford, a man who had given a lifetime of service to Teviotdale Harriers, told them: "A club which has maintained existence for such a period has proved that it has fulfilled a want and has justified its existence."

Now, all these years later, these words have an even stronger significance and sum up the popularity and comradeship of Teviotdale Harriers.

CLUB TROPHY WINNERS

TEVIOTDALE HARRIERS' CUP

Record—I. ELLIOT, 1975. 14 mins. 28 secs.

Senior men—course: 4 laps of Hawick Moor racecourse—3 miles.

1894—J. Ferguson
1895—R. Christie
1896—G. A. Kyle
1897—R. Christie
1898—A. T. Hunter
1899—J. J. Turnbull
1900—J. G. Anderson
1901—G. L. McDonald
1902—R. J. Blake
1903—R. Wilson
1904—O. S. Lawson
1905—J. S. Halliday
1906—A. B. Hobkirk
1907—C. Moffat
1908—J. S. Turnbull
1909—W. Boyd
1910—R. Grierson
1911—T. Lawrence
1912—J. Miller
1913—J. Gordon
1914—W. Boyd
1920—J. Armstrong
1921—J. Menzies
1922—V. Somerville
1923—H. Grieve
1924—G. R. Innes
1925—W. D. Little
1926—R. Lynn
1927—R. E. E. Stewart
1928—J. McCall
1929—E. Taylor
1930—A. Kyle
1931—W. J. Newbigging
1932—G. Armstrong
1933—A. Fox
1934—G. Lumsden
1935—A. Valentine
1936—F. W. Innes
1937—J. A. Brown
1938—D. Jeffrey
1939—G. P. Turnbull
1947—J. Hunter
1948—J. M. Leyden
1949—G. P. Turnbull
1950—G. Murray
1951—G. P. Turnbull
1952—J. R. W. Veitch
1953—R. Rorrison
1954—G. McDavid
1955—W. G. Yule
1956—J. W. Douglas
1957—W. McLeod
1958—R. Wharton
1959—V. Law
1960—D. Jeffrey
1961—R. A. Renton
1962—A. C. Douglas
1963—E. Logan
1964—W. Riddell
1965—W. Riddell
1966—D. Riddell
1967—J. C. Douglas
1968—W. G. Yule
1969—J. W. Raeburn
1970—W. G. Yule
1971—I. Elliot
1972—W. Lindsay
1973—W. G. Yule
1974—W. Lindsay
1975—H. Wear
1976—G. Scott
1977—G. Meikle
1978—J. D. Fairgrieve
1979—S. Barker
1980—F. Cannon
1981—S. Barker
1982—W. Knox
1983—N. Dalgetty
1984—P. Haddock
1985—B. Duff
1986—K. Logan
1987—G. Moyes
1988—B. Gibb

CROSS-COUNTRY CHAMPIONSHIP
CAMPBELL TROPHY

Record—A. WALKER, 1985. 34 mins. 57 secs.

Senior men—course: Museum in Wilton Lodge Park, Walled Garden, Overhall, Brieryhill, Highchesters, Todshawhaugh, Meadows, "Jooglie Brig," Martin's Bridge, Parkdaill, Museum—7 miles.

1895—J. Pringle
1896—T. Davidson
1897—T. Davidson
1898—A. Learmond
1899—R. Christie
1900—R. Christie
1901—J. McVittie
1902—J. Davidson
1903—R. Wilson
1904—A. J. Grieve
1905—A. J. Grieve
1906—J. S. Halliday
1907—A. J. Grieve
1908—A. J. Grieve
1909—J. K. Burns
1910—R. Grierson
1911—A. Anderson
1912—T. Hamilton
1913—J. Grierson
1914—T. Hamilton
1920—R. O. Smith
1921—A. McPhail
1922—D. L. Erskine
1923—D. L. Erskine
1924—D. L. Erskine
1925—D. L. Erskine
1926—D. L. Erskine
1927—J. Telfer
1928—J. Telfer
1929—R. E. E. Stewart
1930—A. Barker
1931—A. Barker
1932—A. Kyle
1933—A. Kyle
1934—A. Turner
1935—A. Turner
1936—A. Kyle
1937—P. Armstrong
1938—J. A. Brown
1939—W. L. Smith
1947—W. Knox
1948—J. Hogg
1949—D. J. Campbell
1950—D. J. Campbell
1951—D. J. Campbell
1952—R. Wilkinson
1953—H. Lawrence
1954—H. Lawrence
1955—H. Lawrence
1956—H. Lawrence
1957—K. Borthwick
1958—J. Jack and R. A. Renton
1959—J. Jack
1960—J. Jack
1961—W. B. Mather
1962—J. C. Douglas
1963—J. C. Douglas
1964—J. C. Douglas
1965—J. C. Douglas
1966—J. C. Douglas
1967—J. W. Raeburn
1968—W. B. Mather
1969—J. W. Raeburn
1970—G. Meikle
1971—I. Elliot
1972—K. Ballantyne
1973—A. Samuel
1974—A. Samuel
1975—A. Samuel
1976—A. Samuel
1977—A. Samuel
1978—J. Murray
1979—M. Elsdon
1980—M. Elsdon
1981—B. Emmerson
1982—B. Emmerson
1983—B. Emmerson
1984—A. Walker
1985—A. Walker
1986—A. Walker
1987—B. Emmerson
1988—B. Emmerson

LANGHEUGH TROPHY

Record—J. C. DOUGLAS, 1965. 27 mins. 44 secs.

Senior men—course: Waterfall in Wilton Lodge Park, Walled Garden, Scawmill, Whitehaugh, Borthaugh Cover, Overhall, Walled Garden—6 miles.

1931-2—J. M. Leyden
1932-3—T. H. Brydon
1933-4—J. Campbell
1934-5—W. Broatch
1935-6—T. H. Jamieson
1936-7—G. Cowban
1937-8—J. A. Brown
1939—P. Armstrong
1947—No race
1948—J. Hunter
1949—R. Campbell
1950—K. Borthwick
1951—R. Beattie
1952—G. P. Turnbull
1953—R. Scott
1954—R. Scott
1955—A. Oliver
1956—M. T. Shankie
1957—R. Wharton
1958—J. M. Hamilton
1959—W. G. Yule
1960—W. B. Mather
1961—G. F. Meikle
1962—M. Telford
1963—D. Riddell
1964—R. Wharton
1965—J. C. Douglas
1966—W. G. Yule
1967—G. Richardson
1968—M. Dodds
1969—G. F. Meikle
1970—G. Moyes
1971—I. Elliot
1972—J. Marsh
1973—B. Gibson
1974—W. Lindsay
1975—J. Marsh
1976—B. Turnbull
1977—N. Taylor
1978—J. Murray
1979—I. Elliot
1980—G. F. Meikle
1981—D. Riddell
1982—I. Elliot
1983—J. Knox
1984—I. Elliot
1985—A. Clyne
1986—K. Elliot
1987—J. Marsh
1988—J. Marsh

WILL CLARK MEMORIAL TROPHY

Senior men—course: Haugh (Burns Club corner), Avenue, Waterfall, Walled Garden, Dunk, Laurie Bridge, Avenue, Haugh—$2\frac{1}{4}$ miles (run on Burns Club Trophy day).

1976—B. Gibson
1977—A. Oliver
1978—F. Cannon
1979—D. Clyne
1980—A. Curruthers
1981—P. Haddock
1982—A. Renwick
1983—S. Bennett
1984—A. Carruthers
1985—J. Darcy
1986—A. Clyne
1987—C. Nichol
1988—K. Logan

JUBILEE TROPHY

Record—I. ELLIOT, 1976. 20 mins. 30 secs.

Senior men—course: Haugh, Avenue, Wilton Burn, Borthaugh Cover, Martin's Bridge, Fisherman's Walk, Dunk, Spetchman's Haugh, Laurie Bridge, Avenue, Haugh—3¾ miles.

1939—B. Smith
1947—W. Knox
1948—W. Read
1949—J. Fox
1950—J. Elliot
1951—W. Read
1952—R. Wilkinson
1953—R. Dryden
1954—R. Dryden
1955—K. Borthwick
1956—G. Moyes
1957—W. Wright
1958—G. Wright
1959—D. Riddell
1960—G. F. Meikle
1961—W. B. Mather
1962—A. Moody
1963—J. M. Hamilton
1964—W. McLeod
1965—J. C. Douglas
1966—G. F. Meikle
1967—A. J. Roden
1968—J. B. Huggan
1969—J. W. Raeburn
1970—G. Richardson
1971—G. F. Meikle
1972—A. Samuel
1973—B. Turnbull
1974—B. Turnbull
1975—G. F. Meikle
1976—I. Elliot
1977—J. Murray
1978—A. Lauder
1979—R. Hodgins
1980—N. Hall
1981—N. Dalgetty
1982—J. Marsh
1983—A. Fair
1984—W. Knox
1985—K. Elliot
1986—A. Fair
1987—W. Knox
1988—J. Darcy

GLENCAIRN TROPHY

First Veteran in Cup Race

1980—G. Meikle
1981—G. Meikle
1982—G. Meikle
1983—D. Riddell
1984—A. Anderson
1985—G. Moyes
1986—G. Moyes
1987—D. Riddell
1988—G. Moyes

ERSKINE TROPHY

Championship Sealed Handicap

1979—D. Clyne and D. Hunter
1980—A. Renwick
1981—C. Hume
1982—J. Marsh
1983—N. Taylor
1984—F. Cannon
1985—B. Fraser
1986—A. Reid
1987—A. Reid
1988—B. Law

MENZIES TROPHY

Record—C. HUME, 1985. 22 mins. 02 secs.

Senior men—course: Victoria Road, Avenue, Walled Garden, Wilton Burn, Borthaugh, Woodfoot, Branxholme Bridge, Martin's Bridge, Buccleuch Road, Haugh—5 miles.

1939—J. Scott
1947—J. W. Douglas
1948—G. Brunton
1949—B. M. Murray
1950—B. M. Murray
1951—M. Richarson
1952—J. Carruthers
1953—H. Lawrence
1954—J. Carruthers
1955—G. Wright
1956—W. Riddell
1957—R. K. Harley
1958—R. Wilkinson
1959—M. T. Shankie
1960—J. Jack
1961—R. K. Harley
1962—J. C. Douglas
1963—G. Tait
1964—G. Murray
1965—J. Newbigging
1966—A. Oliver
1967—A. Oliver
1968—W. Lindsay
1969—A. Samuel
1970—N. Taylor
1971—K. D. Ballantyne
1972—S. Lunn
1973—W. Lindsay
1974—R. Hodgins
1975—A. Samuel
1976—M. Wylie
1977—J. Bouglas
1978—A. Oliver
1979—A. Samuel
1980—D. Hunter
1981—B. Emmerson
1982—D. Riddell
1983—S. Barker
1984—A. Walker
1985—C. Hume
1986—D. Cavers
1987—R. Hall
1988—A. Reid

CHRISTIE CUP

Record—J. C. DOUGLAS, 1966. 11 mins. 7 secs.

Senior men/juniors—course: Victoria Road, Waterfall in Wilton Lodge Park, Walled Garden, "Dunk," Langlands Bridge, Spetchman's Haugh, Laurie Bridge, Avenue, Haugh—2¼ miles.

1964—G. Moyes
1965—J. W. Raeburn
1966—F. Cannon
1967—W. Hogg
1968—J. Marsh
1969—J. W. Raeburn
1970—J. Murray
1971—A. Samuel
1972—G. Moyes
1973—A. Montgomery
1974—D. Blues
1975—W. Riddell

From 1976 this trophy was run as a 3000 metres event (see track section).

JUNIOR SECTION

JUNIOR CHAMPIONSHIP

B. M. MURRAY TROPHY

Record—B. TURNBULL, 1973. 15 mins. 34 secs.

Senior boys/youths—course: Museum in Wilton Lodge Park, Walled Garden, Overhall, Wilton Burn, Borthaugh, Martin's Bridge, Spetchman's Haugh, Laurie Bridge, Bowling Green—3 miles.

1925—G. Harrower
1926—P. Kerr
1927—R. Leithead
1928—T. Jamieson
1929—A. Laidlaw and
W. Newbigging
1930—W. Campbell
1931—R. Richardson
1932—R. Richardson
1933—J. Harrower
1934—W. Smith
1935—T. Aitken
1936—No race
1937—J. Crawford
1938—B. Smith
1939—B. Smith
1947—W. Johnson
1948—G. Brunton
1949—D. Campbell
1950—D. Campbell
1951—D. Campbell
1952—J. Jack
1953—J. Jack
1954—J. Jack
1955—A. Amos
1956—D. A. Oliver
1957—R. K. Harley
1958—W. Ferguson
1959—D. Riddell
1960—R. Jeffrey
1961—J. C. Douglas
1962—J. Raeburn
1963—J. Raeburn
1964—J. Raeburn
1965—W. Nichol
1966—B. Gibson
1967—I. Elliot
1968—N. Taylor
1969—J. Marsh
1970—A. Taylor
1971—J. Marsh
1972—S. Lunn
1973—B. Turnbull
1974—K. Hill
1975—K. Hill
1976—B. Neilson
1977—A. Lauder
1978—A. Lauder
1979—C. Swailes
1980—P. Robertson
1981—A. Pender
1982—C. Nichol
1983—C. Nichol
1984—C. Nichol
1985—C. Nichol
1986—B. Law
1987—C. Murphy
1988—C. Murphy

JUNIOR CUP

Record—A. MOODY, 1961. 7 mins. 27 secs.

Senior boys/youths—course: 2 laps of Hawick Moor racecourse—$1\frac{1}{2}$ miles.

1926—T. Helm
1927—D. Thomson
1928—J. B. Nichol
1929—A. Laidlaw
1930—G. Turnbull
1931—J. Nichol
1932—J. Harrower
1933—W. Smith
1934—W. Smith
1935—A. Lambert
1936—No race
1937—No race
1938—J. Finnie
1939—A. Richardson
1947—No race
1948—J. Ingles
1949—E. Cunningham
1950—D. Richardson
1951—K. Borthwick
1952—W. Clayton
1953—W. Yule
1954—W. Yule
1955—G. Moyes
1956—D. A. Oliver
1957—R. K. Harley
1958—R. K. Harley
1959—P. Roden
1960—A. Moody
1961—A. Moody
1962—R. Nichol
1963—W. J. Pearce
1964—R. Nichol
1965—T. Borthwick
1966—M. Dodds
1967—I. Elliot
1968—J. Marsh
1969—J. Marsh
1970—J. Marsh
1971—No race
1972—D. Anderson
1973—A. Oliver
1974—M. Wylie
1975—A. Oliver
1976—B. Neilson
1977—R. Smith
1978—C. Hamilton
1979—A. Pender
1980—K. Pringle
1981—K. Pringle
1982—A. Clyne
1983—G. Pringle
1984—D. Riddell
1985—Robert Duff
1986—B. Rudkin
1987—S. Purdie
1988—M. Baillie

M. AND M. TROPHY

Record—G. McCusker, 1983. 6 mins. 1 sec.

Colts/junior boys—course: $1\frac{1}{2}$ laps of Hawick Moor racecourse (run on Cup race day).

1969—B. Millar
1970—S. Lunn
1971—A. Oliver
1972—K. Hill
1973—S. Wilkinson
1974—J. Hogarth
1975—G. Campbell
1976—S. McCrone
1977—B. Smith
1978—D. Rudkin
1979—G. Pringle
1980—C. Murphy
1981—C. Nichol
1982—C. Luke
1983—J. Graham
1984—S. Scott
1985—C. Campbell
1986—K. Murray
1987—G. Rodgerson
1988—C. Rodgerson

COLTS' CHAMPIONSHIP

EX-SERVICEMEN'S CLUB TROPHY

Record—C. MURPHY, 1982. 4 mins. 58 secs.

Colts—course: Museum in Wilton Lodge Park, path via Guthrie Memorial, shelter and tennis courts, Langlands Bridge, Spetchman's Haugh, Laurie Bridge, Museum—¾-mile.

1973—A. Lauder
1974—A. Lauder
1975—N. Baillie
1976—D. Fletcher
1977—B. Smith
1978—S. Riddell
1979—C. Nichol
1980—C. Murphy
1981—C. Murphy
1982—C. Murphy
1983—D. Thomson
1984—J. Shaw
1985—B. Wear
1986—D. Hughes
1987—D. Hughes
1988—M. Wight

BOYS' CHAMPIONSHIP

Record—C. MURPHY, 1984. 7 mins. 56 secs.

Junior boys—course: Museum, Avenue, Park gates, Deanfield, Waterfall in Wilton Lodge Park, Walled Garden path, putting green, Langlands Bridge, Spetchman's Haugh, Laurie Bridge, Museum—1½ miles.

1965—J. Marsh
1966—J. Marsh
1967—J. Marsh
1968—S. Lunn
1969—W. Darling and R. Hume
1970—P. Nichol
1971—A. Oliver
1972—K. Hill
1973—C. Hume
1974—C. Hume
1975—S. Hogg
1976—D. Lauder
1977—P. Robertson
1978—P. Robertson
1979—R. Nichol
1980—R. Law
1981—C. Nichol
1982—G. Pringle
1983—G. McCusker
1984—C. Murphy
1985—S. Rae
1986—B. Wear
1987—B. Wear
1988—D. Hughes

LODGE ST. JAMES 424

Senior boys/youths—course: Haugh, Lawson Bridge, River Teviot path to Langlands Bridge, putting green, Walled Garden path, Waterfall in Wilton Lodge Park, Museum, Avenue, Victoria Road, Haugh—1¾ miles (run on Jubilee Trophy race day).

1985—B. Law
1986—G. Robertson
1987—D. Riddell
1988—C. Pringle

BURNS CLUB TROPHY

Record—I. ELLIOT, 1967. 9 mins. 37 secs.

Junior boys/senior boys/youths—course: Haugh (Burns Club corner), Avenue, Museum, Walled Garden, Langlands Bridge, Spetchman's Haugh, Laurie Bridge, Haugh—1½ miles.

1967—T. Dagg
1968—A. Oliver
1969—I. Reid
1970—S. Lunn
1971—S. Lunn
1972—C. Moxey
1973—A. Oliver
1974—C. Hume
1975—B. Neilson
1976—C. Hume
1977—R. Smith
1978—D. Gray
1979—D. Crawford
1980—R. Armstrong
1981—C. Hamilton
1982—G. McCusker
1983—B. Law
1984—M. Skeldon
1985—S. Rae
1986—Ron Duff
1987—M. Bryson
1988—S. Rae

LODGE 111 TROPHY

Senior boys/youths—course: Wilton Lodge Park, bowling green hut, Guthrie Memorial, Violet Woods, Overhall, Hunting Gate, Overhall Cover, Martin's Bridge, Wilton Lodge Park—1¾ miles (run on Langheugh Trophy race day).

1980—A. Pender
1981—A. Clyne
1982—C. Nichol
1983—C. Nichol
1984—D. Riddell
1985—C. Murphy
1986—D. Riddell
1987—C. Pringle
1988—B. Wear

BURNFOOT RESIDENTS ASSOCIATION

Junior boys—course: Wilton Lodge Park bowling green hut, Guthrie Memorial, Violet Woods, "Dunk," tennis courts, bowling green—1¾ miles (run on Langheugh Trophy race day).

1979—C. Swailes
1980—R. Law
1981—D. Rudkin
1982—G. Pringle
1983—C. Murphy
1984—C. Campbell
1985—J. Thomson
1986—J. Graham
1987—B. Wear
1988—D. Tait

TRACK CHAMPIONSHIPS

100 YARDS

Record—I. BELL, 1958. 10.4 secs.
J. L. COLTMAN, 1959. R. I. C. DIROM, 1964.

1926—J. Clark
1927—H. Innes
1928—I. Sutherland
1929—I. Sutherland
1930—R. E. Scott
1931—I. Sutherland
1932—I. Sutherland
1933—A. Armstrong
1934—I. Sutherland
1935—R. E. Scott
1936—R. E. Scott
1937—R. E. Scott
1938—G. Stanger
1939—R. Turnbull
1947—S. Thomson
1948—G. Skedd
1949—R. Hume
1950—R. Hume
1951—W. Wallace
1952—H. Murphy
1953—G. Gibb
1954—H. Murphy
1955—I. Bell
1956—I. Bell
1957—W. Gray
1958—I. Bell
1959—J. L. Coltman
1960—J. L. Coltman
1961—V. Law
1962—D. Riddell
1963—D. Riddell
1964—R. I. C. Dirom
1965—J. C. Douglas
1966—F. Cannon
1967—F. Cannon
1968—F. Cannon
1969—F. Cannon

SCOTT TROPHY

100 METRES

Record—D. McGIBBON, 1972. 11.4 secs.

1970—F. Cannon
1971—D. McGibbon
1972—D. McGibbon
1973—D. Richardson
1974—B. Gibb
1975—B. Gibb
1976—B. Gibb
1977—N. Anderson
1978—B. Gibb
1979—B. Gibb
1980—B. Gibb
1981—B. Gibb
1982—B. Gibb
1983—B. Gibb
1984—B. Gibb
1985—B. Gibb
1986—N. Dalgetty
1987—B. Gibb
1988—B. Gibb

ONE MILE

Record—R. K. HARLEY, 1961. 4 mins. 16.4 secs.

1926—G. Harrower
1927—G. Harrower
1928—G. Harrower
1929—G. Harrower
1930—A. Barker
1931—A. Barker
1932—J. Harrower
1933—J. Harrower
1934—G. Turnbull
1935—P. Armstrong
1936—P. Armstrong
1937—P. Armstrong
1938—P. Armstrong
1939—W. Knox
1947—J. G. Smith
1948—J. Hogg
1949—D. Campbell
1950—D. Campbell
1951—K. Borthwick
1952—R. Wilkinson
1953—D. Campbell
1954—D. Campbell
1955—D. Campbell
1956—D. Campbell and J. Jack
1957—J. Jack
1958—J. Jack
1959—J. Jack
1960—J. Jack
1961—R. K. Harley
1962—J. C. Douglas
1963—J. R. Wilson
1964—J. R. Wilson
1965—J. C. Douglas
1966—J. C. Douglas
1967—I. Elliot
1968—I. Elliot
1969—F. Cannon

1500 METRES

Record—A. WALKER, 1985. 4 mins. 5.4 secs.

1970—I. Elliot
1971—J. Marsh
1972—No race
1973—A. Samuel
1974—A. Samuel
1975—J. Fairgrieve
1976—B. Gibb
1977—No race
1978—D. Clyne
1979—N. Hall
1980—N. Hall
1981—B. Emmerson
1982—N. Hall
1983—C. Nichol
1984—M. Davidson
1985—A. Walker
1986—A. Walker
1987—K. Logan
1988—K. Logan

CHRISTIE CUP

3000 METRES (YOUTHS AND SENIORS)

1976—R. Hodgins
1977—A. Lauder
1978—D. Clyne
1979—P. Cairns
1980—R. Law
1981—C. Nichol
1982—G. McCusker, snr.
1983—D. Rudkin
1984—M. Davidson
1985—D. Carruthers
1986—R. Duff
1987—D. Clyne

REFUGE ASSURANCE TROPHY

3000 METRES (JUNIOR BOYS/SENIOR BOYS)

1987—D. Hughes

COLTMAN CHALLENGE CUP

Presented to most outstanding track athlete of the season

1965—J. C. Douglas
1966—J. C. Douglas
1967—Elizabeth Jarvis
1968—J. Raeburn
1969—I. Glendinning
1970—I. Elliot
1971—K. Anderson and C. Biddle
1972—D. McGibbon
1973—C. Hume
1974—B. Gibb
1975—C. Hume
1976—Alison Campbell
1977—I. Borthwick and A. Lauder
1978—Angela Bennett
1979—Pauline Cairns
1980—Pauline Cairns
1981—B. Emmerson
1982—C. Nichol
1983—C. Nichol
1984—Angela McClure
1985—Joan Anderson
1986—A. Walker
1987—Joan Anderson

LADIES' SECTION

LADIES' CHAMPIONSHIP

BORTHWICK TROPHY

Record—P. CAIRNS, 1979. 8 mins. 54 secs.

Intermediate/senior women—course: Museum, Avenue, Park Gates, Deanfield, Waterfall in Wilton Lodge Park, Walled Garden path, putting green, Langlands Bridge, Spetchman's Haugh, Laurie Bridge, Museum—1½ miles.

1964—E. Petrie
1965—E. Petrie
1966—A. Wilcox
1967—J. Johnston
1968—E. Petrie
1969—M. McHugh
1970—S. Thomson
1971—M. Oliver
1972—R. Telfer
1973—K. Anderson
1974—B. Geddes
1975—B. Geddes
1976—A. Campbell
1977—A. Campbell
1978—A. Campbell
1979—P. Cairns
1980—P. Cairns
1981—P. Cairns
1982—P. Cairns
1983—M. Thomson
1984—A. McClure
1985—K. Wear
1986—J. Murray
1987—J. Anderson
1988—J. Anderson

GIRLS' CHAMPIONSHIP

DOUGLAS TROPHY

Record—J. ANDERSON, 1985. 5 mins. 17 secs.

Minor girls/girls—course: Museum in Wilton Lodge Park, path via Guthrie Memorial, shelter and tennis courts, Langlands Bridge, Spetchman's Haugh, Laurie Bridge, Museum—¾-mile.

1975—L. Renwick
1976—P. Cairns
1977—P. Cairns
1978—D. Irvine
1979—S. Cumming
1980—J. Renwick
1981—S. Douglas
1982—D. Yellowlees
1983—D. Yellowlees
1984—J. Anderson
1985—J. Anderson
1986—J. Anderson
1987—S. Purdie
1988—S. Purdie

LADIES' CHALLENGE TROPHY

Record—J. ANDERSON, 1987. 6 mins. 31 secs.

Intermediate/senior ladies—course: 1½ laps of Hawick Moor racecourse (run on Cup race day).

1978—P. Cairns
1979—N. McCraw
1980—J. McLeod
1981—J. McLeod
1982—L. MacPherson
1983—L. Martin
1984—L. Martin
1985—J. Murray
1986—K. Wear
1987—J. Anderson
1988—M. Parker

LODGE 111 TROPHY

Record—P. CAIRNS, 1980. 10 mins. 4 secs.

Intermediate/senior ladies—course: Wilton Lodge Park bowling green hut, Guthrie Memorial, Violet Woods, "Dunk," tennis courts, bowling green—1¾ miles (run on Langheugh Trophy race day).

1979—D. Irvine
1980—S. Cumming
1981—S. Cumming
1982—D. Irvine
1983—L. MacPherson
1984—J. Anderson
1985—L. MacPherson
1986—L. Martin
1987—K. Wear
1988—A. Murphy

LADIES JUBILEE TROPHY

Record—J. ANDERSON, 1987. 9 mins. 40 secs.

Intermediate/senior ladies—course: Haugh, Lawson Bridge, River Teviot path to Langlands Bridge, putting green, Walled Garden path, Waterfall in Wilton Lodge Park, Museum, Avenue, Victoria Road, Haugh—1¾ miles.

1981—A. Bennett
1982—M. Douglas
1983—L. Jack
1984—A. McClure
1985—K. Wear
1986—J. Murray
1987—J. Anderson
1988—J. Hewat

FIRE BRIGADE CUP

Record—J. ANDERSON, 1986. 7 mins. 22 secs.

Minor girls/girls—course: Wilton Lodge Park bowling green hut, path via Guthrie Memorial and shelter, bowling green—1 mile (run on Langheugh Trophy race day).

1985—C. Livingston
1986—A. Murphy
1987—J. Scott
1988—S. Purdie

JOHN ELLIOT TROPHY

Record—S. PURDIE, 1987. 4 mins. 21 secs.

Minor girls/girls—course: one lap of Hawick Moor racecourse (run on Cup race day).

1981—F. Thomson
1982—L. Martin
1983—M. Borthwick
1984—K. Mackintosh
1985—S. Wight
1986—A. Irvine
1987—A. Spence
1988—A. Spence

CRAIG DOUGLAS TROPHY

100 METRES (LADIES)

1971—R. Telfer
1972—C. Biddle
1973—C. Biddle
1974—A. Reid
1975—A. Reid
1976—S. Walker
1977—S. Walker
1978—A. Bennett
1979—P. Cairns
1980—P. Cairns
1981—P. Cairns
1982—J. McLeod
1983—J. McLeod
1984—A. McClure
1985—A. McClure
1986—A. McClure
1987—J. Murray
1988—J. Murray

LADIES PAST CAPTAINS

1972-73—R. Telfer
1973-74—M. McHugh
1974-75—A. Reid
1975-76—A. Campbell
1976-77—A. Reid
1977-78—A. Campbell
1978-79—A. Short
1979-80—A. Bennett
1980-81—D. Irvine
1981-82—J. McLeod
1982-83—L. Sayers
1983-84—M. H. Douglas
1984-85—D. Yellowlees
1985-86—A. McClure
1986-87—L. Martin
1987-88—J. Anderson

BORDER CHAMPIONS

This list of Teviotdale Harriers who have been successful in winning a Scottish Border Amateur Athletic Association championship has been obtained from various sources, apology is made for any omissions or errors as no official records are kept.

The Langlands Trophy was presented to the S.B.A.A.A. by Sir Thomas Henderson, Langlands, Hawick, for the 220 yards championship, now the 200 metres. The trophy was first competed for at the Hawick Y.M.C.A. Sports in the Volunteer Park in 1921.

1905—A. J. Grieve: mile
1906—A. J. Grieve: mile
1907—A. J. Grieve: mile
1908—A. J. Grieve: mile
1909—A. J. Grieve: mile
1910—A. J. Grieve: mile
R. H. Burton: 440y
1911—W. R. Sutherland: 100y, 220y
R. H. Burton: 440y
1912—W. R. Sutherland: 100y, 220y
R. H. Burton: 440y
1913—W. R. Sutherland: 100y, 220y
R. H. Burton: 440y
1914—W. R. Sutherland: 100y, 220y
1920—J. B. N. Ballantyne: 100y, 220y, 440y
1921—W. R. Chisholm: 220y
1922—W. R. Chisholm: 220y
1924—H. Innes: 100y
1926—I. Sutherland: 100y
1927—I. Sutherland: 100y, 220y
1928—I. Sutherland: 100y, 220y, 440y
I. Carruthers/H. Innes: high jump
1929—I. Sutherland: 100y, 220y
I. Carruthers: discus, high jump
P. McDonald: 440y
1930—I. Sutherland: 220y
A. Valentine: 440y, 880y
A. Barker: mile
G. Taylor: high jump, 120y hurdles
1931—I. Sutherland: 100y
A. Valentine: 880y
A. B. Armstrong: 220y
P. McDonald: 440y
1932—A. Valentine: 440y, 880y
1933—F. J. McQuade: 880y
P. Armstrong: mile
I. Carruthers: high jump
A. J. Sangster: shot

Border Champions (continued)

1934—P. Armstrong: mile
I. Sutherland: 100y, 220y
A. J. Sangster: shot

1935—I. Sutherland: 100y 220y
P. Armstrong: mile

1936—J. R. Hogg: 100y
R. E. Scott: 220y
A. J. Sangster: shot
P. Armstrong: mile

1937—R. E. Scott: 100y, 220y
T. Young: 220y (youths)
P. Armstrong: mile
A. J. Sangster: shot

1938—G. Stanger: 100y
T. Young: 880y
P. Armstrong: mile

1939—W. Knox: 880y, mile
J. Ross: 220y (youths), 100y
T. G. Young: 440y
W. Thompson: 220y

1947—G. Sked: 100y, 220y
J. Hogg: 880y

1949—R. Hume: 100y
S. Thomson: 220y
A. Richardson: 440y
J. Hogg: 880y
B. M. Murray: 3 mile
A. P. McIntyre: high jump

1950—B. M. Murray: 3 mile

1951—J. Grierson: 440y, 880y

1952—I. Bell: 220y (youths)
W. Thomson: javelin

1953—D. J. Campbell: mile

1954—D. J. Campbell: mile

1955—D. J. Campbell: mile

1956—I. Bell: 100y, 220y
H. Lawrence: 3 mile

1957—I. Bell: 100y, 220y
W. Gray: 220y (junior)

1958—I. Bell: 100y, 220y, 440y
G. Wright: 880y
R. Renton: mile
J. Jack: 3 mile
W. Britee: discus
O. Grant: shot
S. Montgomery: 880y (junior)

Border Champions (continued)

1959—J. L. Coltman: 100y, 220y
J. Jack: 3 mile
P. Roden: 880y (junior)
G. Wright: 880y
R. Renton: mile
1960—J. L. Coltman: 100y
J. Jack: mile
R. Renton: 3 mile
I. Weir. shot, discus
C. Douglas: 880y (junior)
1961—K. Harley: mile, 3 mile
I. Weir: shot, discus, hammer
D. Forrest: hop, step and jump
K. Brydon: 100y (junior), 220y (junior)
C. Douglas: 880y (junior), mile (junior)
1962—R. Gaunt: 220y (youths)
P. Roden: 880y, mile
B. Mather: 3 mile
I. Weir: shot, discus, hammer
D. Forrest: hop, step and jump
1963—C. Douglas: 880y, mile
J. Raeburn: mile (junior)
D. Forrest: broad jump, triple jump
1964—C. Douglas: 440y, 880y, 3 mile
D. Henry: 880y (junior)
I. Weir: discus, hammer
R. Wilson: mile
I. Williams: long jump
R. Sykes: shot
J. Raeburn: mile (junior)
1965—C. Douglas: 220y, 440y, 880y, mile
F. Cannon: 100y (junior), 220y (junior)
A. Drummond: shot
I. Elliot: 880y (youths)
J. Buchan: discus
D. Forrest: broad jump, triple jump
1966—C. Douglas: 100y, 440y, 880y, mile
F. Cannon: 220y
G. Richardson: mile (junior)
I. Elliot: 220y (youths)
J. Raeburn: 3 mile
D. Forrest: long jump, triple jump
1967—F. Cannon: 220y
I. Elliot: 100y (junior), 880y (junior), mile (junior)
B. Nichols: javelin (junior)
N. Taylor: 880y (youths)
J. Raeburn: 3 mile
A. Drummond: hammer

Border Champions (continued)

1968—F. Cannon: 220y, 440y, 880y
I. Glendinning: 100y (youths)
I. Elliot: 220y (junior), 880y (junior), mile, 3 mile
A. Drummond: hammer

1969—F. Cannon: 100y, 220y, 880y
I. Glendinning: 100y (junior)
J. Raeburn: mile, 3 mile

1970—I. Glendinning: 100y (junior), 220y (junior), 100y, 220y
I. Elliot: 1500m, 3 miles
F. Cannon: 400m, 800m
A. Taylor: 800m (youths)

1971—S. Lunn: 1500m (juniors)

1972—J. Marsh: 1500m (junior)

1973—R. Crawford: 800m (junior)
J. Marsh: 1500m (junior), javelin
W. Yule: discus

1974—A. Campbell: 400m (girls)

1975—B. Gibb: 100m (junior)
B. Neilson: 800m (boys)

1976—B. Gibb: 200m
G. Meikle: 5000m

1977—B. Gibb: 100m
N. Anderson: 400m
N. Hall: 5000m

1978—B. Gibb: 100m, 200m
D. Clyne: 400m
A. Samuel: 5000m

1979—M. Elsdon: 5000m

1981—B. Emmerson: 5000m

1982—J. McLeod: long jump (girls)
D. Yellowlees: 800m (girls)
C. Nichol: 800m (senior boys)

1983—C. Waldie: 100m (junior boys), long jump (junior boys)
C. Murphy: 800m (junior boys)
C. Nichol: 1500m (youths)

1984—C. Campbell: 800m (junior boys)
A. McClure: 200m (junior ladies)
J. Anderson: 800m (girls)

1985—A. McClure: 100m, 200m (intermediate ladies)
A. Goodfellow: 100m (girls)
J. Anderson: 800m (girls)
B. Law: 1500m (youths)
D. Yellowlees: high jump (intermediate ladies)

Border Champions (continued)

1986—L. Martin: 100m, 200m, shot (senior ladies)
A. McClure: 100m, 200m (intermediate ladies)
A. Murphy: 800m (girls)
C. Campbell: 800m (senior boys)
L. Hogg: 800m (junior ladies)
J. Murray: 800m (intermediate ladies)
R. Hall: 5000m
K. Murray: 100m (girls)
A. Fair: 3000m steeplechase
K. Murray: 800m hurdles (senior boys)
1987—D. Cavers: 3000m steeplechase, 5000m
S. Purdie: 800m (girls)
L. Hogg: 800m (junior ladies)
M. Bryson: 800m (youths)
J. Murray: 800m (intermediate ladies)
J. Hogg: long jump (junior ladies)
1988—D. Cavers: 3000m steeplechase, 5000m
D. Hughes: 800m (junior boys)
S. Spence: 800m (girls)
M. Bailey: 800m (senior boys)
A. Murphy: 800m (junior ladies)
A. Bell: discus, javelin (senior boys)

Teviotdale 1987-88 captains Colin Pringle (junior) and Joan Anderson (lady) model the centenary year T-shirts which were supplied by sportswear leaders Lyle & Scott of Hawick. Included in the photograph is Lyle & Scott promotions manager Ian Jackson. Though not a runner himself, Ian has a family connection with athletics. His wife Jean was a Kelso High School champion and her father was Scottish sprint champion Ian Sutherland (see pages 16, 17, 26). Her brother Ian (see pages 87, 88) was also a prominent member of the Hawick club.

PAST CAPTAINS

1889 —J. R. Purdom
1889-90—G. H. Wilson
1890-91—J. W. Glenny
1891-92—G. S. Porteous
1892-93—D. S. McBean
1893-94—R. Bowie
1894-95—R. Thomson
1895-96—Alex. Bell
1896-97—G. L. McDonald
1897-98—G. L. McDonald
1898-99—R. Christie
1899-00—R. Christie
1900-01—R. Christie
1901-02—J. Davidson
1902-03—J. Davidson
1903-04—J. Davidson
1904-05—J. McVittie
1905-06—W. P. Gaylor
1906-07—O. S. Lawson
1907-08—S. Marchbank
1908-09—J. S. Halliday
1909-10—W. Boyd
1910-11—D. Alston
1911-12—D. Alston
1912-13—T. Hamilton
1913-14—T. Cuthbertson
1919-20—Wm. Boyd
1920-21—J. Whitelaw
1921-22—R. Crawford
1922-23—G. R. Innes
1923-24—J. H. Scott
1924-25—J. E. Duff
1925-26—J. Menzies
1926-27—R. E. E. Stewart
1927-28—W. Caldwell
1928-29—F. Elliot
1929-30—J. Campbell
1930-31—P. Kerr
1931-32—T. H. Jamieson
1932-33—G. Oliver
1933-34—T. H. Brydon
1934-35—F. W. Innes
1935-36—G. Lumsden
1936-37—A. Turner
1937-38—J. Scott
1938-39—G. E. Stenhouse
1939-40—J. M. Leyden
1946-47—T. H. Brydon
1947-48—J. A. C. Murray
1948-49—J. S. Reid
1949-50—A. Richardson
1950-51—G. Murray
1951-52—J. R. W. Veitch
1952-53—J. Elliot
1953-54—R. Wilkinson
1954-55—H. Lawrence
1955-56—G. Wright
1956-57—J. Douglas
1957-58—M. T. Shankie
1958-59—V. Law
1959-60—J. Jack
1960-61—J. M. Hamilton
1961-62—P. C. Roden
1962-63—W. B. Mather
1963-64—R. K. Harley
1964-65—J. C. Douglas
1965-66—G. F. Meikle
1966-67—W. Riddell
1967-68—W. G. Yule
1968-69—J. W. Raeburn
1969-70—J. B. Huggan
1970-71—I. Elliot
1971-72—A. Samuel
1972-73—N. H. Taylor
1973-74—J. P. Marsh
1974-75—H. Wear
1975-76—R. Hodgins
1976-77—A. Oliver
1977-78—J. Murray
1978-79—J. Bouglas
1979-80—S. Barker
1980-81—B. Emmerson
1981-82—B. Gibb
1982-83—N. Hall
1983-84—N. Dalgetty
1984-85—A. Carruthers
1985-86—M. Davidson
1986-87—A. Walker
1987-88—A. Renwick

CLUB MEMBERS

Members of Teviotdale Harriers in the 1987-88 season:—

HON. VICE-PRESIDENTS—J. O. Brown, J. Cochrane, J. L. Coltman, A. C. Douglas, N. Douglas, L. Elliot, D. A. Forrest, J. Fox, J. M. Hamilton, J. Hogg, W. Knox, V. Law, H. Lawrence, A. Oliver, G. Oliver, A. Richardson, D. Scott, J. G. S. Smith, Mrs J. Taylor, M. Wear, R. Wilkinson, J. Winslow, W. G. Yule.

MINOR GIRLS—A. McLaren, J. Scott, S. Spence, K. Stenhouse, R. Stenhouse.

GIRLS—S. Bailey, A. Irvine, S. McLaren, S. Purdie, C. Reid, J. Renwick, K. Robertson, A. Spence, P. Yule, A. Zavaroni.

JUNIOR WOMEN—J. Anderson, S. Hair, D. Irvine, K. McGeorge, A. Murphy, M. Traynor.

INTERMEDIATE LADIES—J. Hewat, L. Young.

SENIOR LADIES—J. Anderson, L. Macpherson, F. McNairn, J. Murray, P. Murray, M. Parker, *M. Spence, *D. Yellowlees.

COLTS—M. Brown, M. Brown, G. Dalgleish, G. Douglas, B. Hughes, D. Linton, G. McAuley, C. Murray, D. Stewart, S. Taylor, M. Wight, S. Watson, G. Yule.

JUNIOR BOYS—G. Froud, S. Hogg, D. Hughes, J. Hughes, C. Rodgerson, G. Scott, S. Scott, N. Stewart, D. Tait, G. Young.

SENIOR BOYS—C. Campbell, C. Pringle, S. Purdie, G. Riddell, B. Wear.

YOUTHS—M. Bailey, M. Bryson, Rob Duff, Ron Duff, C. Murphy, S. Rae, G. Robertson, B. Rudkin.

SENIOR MEN—J. Amos, S. Amos, S. Barker, S. Bennett, D. Bett, J. Bouglas, F. Brown, T. Brown, F. Cannon, *A. Carruthers, D. Carruthers, A. Casson, D. Cavers, R. Chlopas, D. Clyne, A. Coltman, R. Cranston, N. Dalgetty, J. Darcy, M. Davidson, R. Duff, I. Elliot, K. Elliot, B. Emmerson, A. Fair, *M. Fox, B. Fraser, B. Gibb, R. Hall, R. Hodgins, *W. Hogg, D. Hunter, W. Knox, B. Law, W. Lindsay, W. Linton, K. Logan, W. Mabon, J. Marsh, M. McClure, D. McMillan, *R. McNairn, R. Mitchell, G. Moyes, C. Moxey, I. Murdie, B. Neilson, C. Nichol, A. Oliver, C. Parr, D. Potts, *W. Pringle, N. Purdie, R. Rae, A. Reid, A. Renwick, Dennis Riddell, Derek Riddell, D. Robson, P. Rodgers, A. Samuel, B. Scott, G. Scott, A. Shankie, I. Sinclair, D. Smith, B. Spence, *C. Stewart, N. Taylor, R. Templeman, M. Tinker, A. Walker.

ASSOCIATE MEMBERS — B. Allison, J. Allison, W. Anderson, W. Anderson, A. Bailey, I. Brennan, S. Burrell, D. Campbell, Mrs M. Coltman, Mrs B. Cummings, Mrs M. Elliot, T. Elliot, R. Froud, S. Froud, N. Gobby, B. Hogg, Mrs T. Hogg, R. Howden, Mrs M. Hughes, B. James, W. Knox, Mrs J. Mabon, W. Mabon, Mrs G. Marsh, Mrs H. Marsh, W. Marsh, Mrs B. McAulay, Miss J. Moscrop, Mrs L. Murray, Mrs S. Purdie, Mrs C. Seath, M. Tierney, M. Watson, D. Wear, Mrs G. Wear, A. Whillans, Mrs E. Wight.

*Non-competing.

Teviotdale Harriers Centenary Committee. They are (back row, left to right)—Grant Moyes, John Hamilton, Jake Coltman, John Marsh and (front row)—Nancy Douglas, Ronnie Pringle and Vic Law.

STAN REID — THE DEVOTED HARRIER

No book about the Harriers would be complete without mentioning Stan Reid. Probably the best known member of Teviotdale, Stan joined as a junior in 1936 and was still running in 1973 when ill-health forced him to finally "hang up his running shoes."

Always the true amateur, winning to Stan came only second to his love for cross-country running with his clubmates. In the days when a trail of paper was used to mark the course before the race, Stan thought nothing of running round with the paper then getting back just in time to take up his place in the handicap for the race itself. He never gave himself a chance by doing this but that was his way. Always popular with the younger members, he was first to give any encouragement that was required.

A great worker for the club, he preferred to do other duties rather than serve on committees, whether it be looking after the clubrooms, especially in frosty weather, book sales, whist drives, sales of work, etc., Stan was there to lend a hand. Before the clubrooms were built, it was Stan who organised training runs from the Baths every Monday and Wednesday night and everyone was made welcome whether they were experienced runners or just beginners.

"Retired"

In 1967 Stan "retired." Following a motor-cycle accident 17 months previously when he broke an ankle, Stan found the injury a great handicap and reluctantly was forced to give up active participation in the Harriers. To mark his "retirement" a "farewell run" was organised when a number of his clubmates turned out and he was also conferred with life membership of Teviotdale.

However, his "retirement" was short-lived and he was soon back among his clubmates. In 1968 he was one of 17 Harriers who took part in a club run from Langholm to Hawick — 22 miles — the longest ever attempted. Five completed the course, they were: Joe Raeburn (2 hrs. 12 mins. 33 secs.), Brian Mather, Alan Roden, Willie Lindsay and Rob Wharton.

The Christie Cup race that year included "veterans" Willie Lindsay (40), W. "Fush" Hogg (50), Arthur Oliver (42) — and yes, Stan Reid (46).

In 1970, following a good performance in a 6-mile road-race for "vets" at Bolton where Willie finished 2nd; Arthur, 17th; and Stan, 25th; the trio competed at Leeds where Willie won by half-a-mile, Arthur was 14th and Stan, 21st. Their next "outing" was an invitation to compete in the European International Veterans' Championships at Leiden, Holland. Against runners from five countries, Willie, who ran for Scotland in Spain in 1955 when a member of Edinburgh Southern, won the race, with Arthur, 32nd and Stan, 59th.

The moment which gave Stan the greatest pride was in 1970 when he was one of those who carried the Queen's message from Canada through the streets of Hawick on its way to the Commonwealth Games in Edinburgh.

Sadly, in 1973, due to ill-health, he was forced to call it a day. His many friends showed their appreciation at a special function in his honour when he was presented with a suitably inscribed silver salver and crystal glasses after 37 years with the club. The person who made the presentation that night was Gideon Lumsden, the man who had paid Stan's first membership and introduced him to cross-country running.

Stan died in 1981, aged 59, it is a great pity he did not live to see the centenary of his much-loved club.

Winners of the European International Veterans' Cross-Country race in Holland in 1970 (left to right)—Arthur Oliver, Willie Lindsay (individual winner) and Stan Reid.

Stan Reid (right) being presented with a silver salver by Gid Lumsden to mark his retiral from running. Stan "hung up his years with the club. running shoes" after 37

OFFICIALS AND FAITHFUL SERVANTS

Many clubs, sporting and otherwise, often struggle to find officials but it can safely be said that Teviotdale Harriers have never been in this category. Over the years they have been fortunate in having some hard working servants. No club can function properly without a dedicated committee and this is one of the main reasons why Teviotdale have been at the forefront of Scottish athletics.

Bob Crawford was a name linked with Border athletics for many years. He can be seen on many of the old photographs of the Harriers between the war years and was one of the first members of the Hawick club to be given life membership of the Scottish Borders Amateur Athletic Association. At the Harriers dinner in 1935 he intimated his retirement from the committee. Club president C. C. Murray said of him: "Few Harriers have worked harder for their club than Bob Crawford. He has occupied almost every office in addition to serving on the committee for the past 23 years." Bob was elected president of the S.B.A.A.A. on several occasions — honours he richly deserved.

John Campbell's name is synonymous with Border athletics. After 45 years' service to the sport he received life membership of the S.B.A.A.A. in 1964, an honour bestowed on him by his own club in 1951. For many years he was convener of the Hawick Common-Riding Amateur Games before Teviotdale Harriers took over and was responsible for bringing such world renowned athletes as E. Macdonald Bailey and Derek Ibbotson to the town. John officiated at the 1970 Commonwealth Games in Edinburgh.

Gid Lumsden, Willie Nichol, George Turnbull and Douglas Campbell gave valuable service to the club and their efforts were rewarded with life membership. Willie Knox, Archie Richardson, John Veitch, John Hogg and George Crawford gave their support when it was most needed in the years after the Second World War to get the club back in operation and Tom Gillies, George Stenhouse and George Bell all played their part, long after their running days were over.

At the present time, the club's oldest members — not their age, one may hasten to add — are Arthur Oliver and Jock Carruthers. Both have been involved with the club for nearly 40 years and, like many Teviotdale officials, started on the competitive side. Jock was in road, middle distance and track events, while Arthur, one of the trio of successful veterans mentioned previously, took to the cross-country. The latter is still enjoying his running and has probably taken part in more Scottish Championships than anyone else in the club. Both have held the office of club president. Jock has been honorary president of the Harriers since 1978 and received life membership of the S.B.A.A.A. in 1982.

W. "Barty" Yule and Grant Moyes both joined as juniors in the 1950s, concentrating on cross-country with some measure of success. Grant made a come-back in recent years and among his successes as a "veteran" was his win in the 1987 Cup race — and a very popular holder he proved to be. Over the years Grant has been involved in several duties within the club and "Barty" has served on the committee, held the post of president and has now reached the stage of a grade one starter.

Vic Law started as a sprinter in the early 1950s before moving to cross-country and winning the senior Cup in 1959. A committee member for a number of years, Vic carried out the duties of treasurer for 12 successive seasons from 1972.

R. Wilkinson, a keen Teviotdale Harrier, joined about 1952 and had several track and cross-country successes. Though business commitments took him away from Hawick for some years, Dick returned to the Borders, settling in Innerleithen and so continued his association with Teviotdale. A former S.B.A.A.A. president, he still officiates at club and Eastern District events.

Andy Douglas, older brother of Craig, has contributed much to the Hawick club since being reinstated amateur in 1962 — only two months before he won the senior Cup. He took over as coach to the ladies' section in 1966 and has held such posts as secretary, ladies' secretary and president, as well as president of the S.B.A.A.A.

In 1982, Andy relinquised the office of secretary to his sister Nancy, so retaining the strong Douglas family association with Teviotdale.

When Gala Harriers ceased to function for a spell, George Meikle joined Teviotdale, that was in 1959 and became one of the Hawick club's keenest members, enjoying tremendous success in cross-country events. He was the first to win the Jubilee Trophy four times — first in 1960 and the last in 1974 — and in 1977, at the age of 37, won the Cup race. In winning the Langheugh Trophy in 1980 he became the first to win it three times. On reaching the "veteran" stage, George has now returned to Gala Harriers and has been instrumental in reserecting the club.

Other club members that come to mind who have served Teviotdale well over the years in open competition include Dennis Riddell, Ian Bell, Francis Cannon, Jim Bouglas, Ronnie Hodgins, Norman Taylor, John Marsh and Alan Samuel.

Though not figuring much in prize lists, Ronnie Pringle has devoted a great deal of his time to the administration of club affairs. He first joined Teviotdale in 1952, then, following National Service, took to coaching and rejoined the club in 1975. His involvement in club affairs was such that he was elected president for the 1981-82 season, a post he has held ever since but for one year.

His wife Kathleen joined Teviotdale in 1978 and immediately set to involve herself "behind the scenes."

This husband and wife team extended their participation in athletics to national level and were soon officiating at championship and international meetings. In 1986, both Ronnie and Kathleen were officials at the Commonwealth Games in Edinburgh.

This review of club officials and faithful servants concludes with a man who has taken the name of Teviotdale to the highest level in athletic circles. That person is John Hamilton.

He was a member of Braidburn A.C. prior to coming to work in Hawick in 1956. His active days included winning the Jubilee Trophy in 1963 and the Langheugh Trophy in 1958.

This "adopted Teri" has held the post of club president, treasurer, has been Teviotdale's Eastern District Cross-Country Union representative since 1964 and was president of the S.B.A.A.A. on several occasions.

John set his sights further afield and from 1963 to 1967 was chairman of the E.D.C.C.U., then elected president of the Scottish Cross-Country Union for the 1969-70 season — the first Borderer to be so honoured — and president of the Scottish Amateur Athletic Association in 1981.

From 1979 he has been Scotland's track and cross-country team manager and this has taken him to Switzerland, Ireland, Italy, Poland, Norway, America, Holland, Spain, France, Belgium, Greece, Hungary, Portugal and Israel. In 1986 he was a member of the British Amateur Athletic selection committee and further honours came that year when he was an official at the Commonwealth Games in Edinburgh as assistant team manager.

Left to right: Ronnie Pringle, Kathleen Pringle and John Hamilton.

TEVIOTDALE HARRIERS CLUB OFFICE-BEARERS

As no official records have been kept, the following information has been obtained from various sources, unfortunately it is not complete. It is quite possible in the early years there was no president as the captain and secretary were responsible for all club activities.

PAST PRESIDENTS

1889 —
1889-90—
1890-91—
1891-92—
1892-93—G. H. Wilson
1893-94—G. H. Wilson
1894-95—G. H. Wilson
1895-96—G. H. Wilson
1896-97—G. H. Wilson
1897-98—G. H. Wilson
1898-99—G. H. Wilson
1899-00—G. H. Wilson
1900-01—Dr Bannerman
1901-02—
1902-03—
1903-04—
1904-05—
1905-06—
1906-07—
1907-08—
1908-09—
1909-10—
1910-11—
1911-12—
1912-13—
1913-14—
1914-15—
1915-19—War Years
1919-20—C. J. Glenny
1920-21—C. J. Glenny
1921-22—
1922-23—
1923-24—
1924-25—
1925-26—
1926-27—T. Gillies
1927-28—T. Gillies
1928-29—T. Gillies
1929-30—T. Gillies
1930-31—T. Gillies
1931-32—T. Gillies
1932-33—R. Crawford
1933-34—C. C. Murray
1934-35—C. C. Murray
1935-36—C. C. Murray
1936-37—J. Campbell
1937-38—G. T. Harrower
1938-39—G. T. Harrower
1939-40—G. T. Harrower
1940-46—War Years
1946-47—G. T. Harrower
1947-48—G. T. Harrower
1948-49—T. H. Brydon
1949-50—T. H. Brydon
1950-51—
1951-52—G. Lumsden
1952-53—G. Lumsden
1953-54—
1954-55—J. Veitch
1955-56—G. Bell
1956-57—G. Bell
1957-58—G. Bell
1958-59—G. Bell
1959-60—G. Crawford
1960-61—G. Crawford
1961-62—J. Veitch
1962-63—J. Veitch
1963-64—D. J. Campbell
1964-65—D. J. Campbell
1965-66—J. C. Carruthers
1966-67—J. C. Curruthers
1967-68—J. C. Carruthers
1968-69—A. Oliver
1969-70—A. Oliver
1970-71—J. M. Hamilton
1971-72—J. M. Hamilton
1972-73—J. M. Hamilton
1973-74—J. M. Hamilton
1974-75—J. M. Hamilton

Presidents (continued)

1975-76—J. M. Hamilton
1976-77—J. M. Hamilton
1977-78—W. G. Yule
1978-79—W. G. Yule
1979-80—W. G. Yule
1980-81—W. G. Yule
1981-82—R. S. Pringle
1982-83—R. S. Pringle
1983-84—R. S. Pringle
1984-85—A. C. Douglas
1985-86—R. S. Pringle
1986-87—R. S. Pringle
1987-88—R. S. Pringle

PAST JOINT SECRETARY AND TREASURERS

1889 —C. M. Purdom
1889-90—J. Turnbull
1890-91—J. Thomson
1891-92—J. Thomson
1892-93—C. Armstrong
1893-94—T. Davidson
1894-95—T. Davidson
1895-96—T. Davidson
1896-97—T. Davidson
1897-98—T. Davidson
1898-99—T. Davidson
1899-00—T. Davidson
1900-01—
1901-02—
1902-03—T. Davidson
1903-04—T. Davidson
1904-05—G. A. Kyle
1905-06—G. A. Kyle and J. McVittie
1906-07—G. L. McDonald and J. McVittie
1907-08—G. L. McDonald and J. McVittie
1908-09—R. Scott
1909-10—G. L. McDonald and J. McVittie
1910-11—G. L. McDonald and J. Cuthbertson
1911-12—Z. C. Mann and A. Anderson
1912-13—Z. C. Mann and A. Anderson
1913-14—J. Grierson and A. Anderson
1914-15—J. Grierson and J. McAllister
1915-19—War Years
1919-20—J. S. Halliday and R. Crawford
1920-21—J. S. Halliday and J. H. Scott
1922-23—
1923-24—
1924-25—W. E. Jack and T. Ferguson
1925-26—
1926-27—J. Menzies and C. C. Murray
1927-28—J. Menzies and C. C. Murray

PAST JOINT SECRETARY/SECRETARIES

1928-29—C. C. Murray
1929-30—J. M. Richardson
1930-31—J. M. Richardson
1931-32—J. M. Richardson
1932-33—J. M. Richardson
1933-34—C. C. Murray and J. Campbell
1934-35—C. C. Murray and J. Campbell

Secretaries (continued)

1935-36—G. Lumsden and
J. Campbell
1936-37—G. Lumsden and
J. Campbell
1937-38—G. Lumsden and
J. Campbell
1938-39—G. Lumsden and
J. Campbell
1939-40—G. Lumsden and
J. Campbell
1940-46—War Years
1946-47—G. Lumsden and
J. Campbell
1947-48—G. Lumsden and
J. Campbell
1948-49—G. Lumsden and
J. Campbell
1949-50—G. Lumsden and
J. Campbell
1950-51—J. Campbell
1951-52—W. Knox and
W. Turnbull
1952-53—D. J. Campbell
1953-54—D. J. Campbell
1954-55—D. J. Campbell
1955-56—D. J. Campbell
1956-57—D. J. Campbell
1957-58—D. J. Campbell
1958-59—D. J. Campbell
1959-60—D. J. Campbell
1960-61—D. J. Campbell
1961-62—D. J. Campbell
1962-63—D. J. Campbell
1963-64—V. Law
1964-65—A. C. Douglas
1965-66—A. C. Douglas
1966-67—A. C. Douglas
1967-68—R. Johnston
1968-69—R. Hodgins
1969-70—R. Hodgins
1970-71—R. Hodgins
1971-72—R. Hodgins
1972-73—N. H. Taylor
1973-74—A. Samuel
1974-75—N. H. Taylor
1975-76—N. H. Taylor
1976-77—A. C. Douglas
1977-78—A. C. Douglas
1978-79—A. C. Douglas
1979-80—A. C. Douglas
1980-81—A. C. Douglas
1981-82—A. C. Douglas
1982-83—Nancy Douglas
1983-84—Nancy Douglas
1984-85—Nancy Douglas
1985-86—Nancy Douglas
1986-87—Nancy Douglas
1987-88—Kathleen Pringle

PAST TREASURERS

1928-29—R. E. E. Stewart
1929-30—R. Crawford
1930-31—R. Crawford
1931-32—R. Crawford
1932-33—R. Crawford
1933-34—G. Oliver
1934-35—J. Menzies
1935-36—J. Menzies
1936-37—J. Menzies
1937-38—J. Menzies
1938-39—J. Menzies
1939-40—H. Nivet
1940-46—War Years
1946-47—H. Nivet
1947-48—J. Hogg
1948-49—J. Hogg
1949-50—J. Hogg
1950-51—E. Murray
1951-52—E. Murray and S. Reid
1952-53—S. Reid
1953-54—
1954-55—
1955-56—G. Wright
1956-57—R. Wilkinson
1957-58—R. Wilkinson
1958-59—J. M. Hamilton

Treasurers (continued)

1959-60—J. M. Hamilton
1960-61—J. M. Hamilton
1961-62—J. M. Hamilton
1962-63—J. M. Hamilton
1963-64—J. M. Hamilton
1964-65—J. M. Hamilton
1965-66—J. M. Hamilton
1966-67—J. M. Hamilton
1967-68—J. M. Hamilton
1968-69—J. M. Hamilton
1969-70—J. M. Hamilton
1970-71—F. McDonald
1971-72—W. G. Yule
1972-73—V. Law
1973-74—V. Law
1974-75—V. Law
1975-76—V. Law
1976-77—V. Law
1977-78—V. Law
1978-79—V. Law
1979-80—V. Law
1980-81—V. Law
1981-82—V. Law
1982-83—V. Law
1983-84—V. Law
1984-85—N. Dalgetty
1985-86—N. Dalgetty
1986-87—N. Dalgetty
1987-88—N. Dalgetty

LIFE-MEMBERS

1895—R. Thomson, Hoylake
1898—A. Bell, Wrexham
1904—T. Davidson, South Africa
1929—G. A. Kyle
1930—Ex-Provost G. H. Wilson, East Grinstead
1931—J. R. Purdom
1937—G. L. McDonald
1938—C. J. Glenny, Deanfield
1948—J. Menzies, Australia
1950—R. Crawford
1951—J. Campbell
1955—G. Lumsden
1955—W. Nichol
1955—G. P. Turnbull
1965—D. J. Campbell
1967—J. S. Reid

S.B.A.A.A. OFFICIALS

This list of Teviotdale Harriers who have been elected leading officials of the S.B.A.A.A. has been obtained from various sources, apology is made for any omissions or errors as no official records are kept.

1897—J. W. Glenny, vice-president
1898—Dr Bannerman, vice-president
1901—J. Thomson, president
T. Davidson, treasurer
1902—J. Thomson, president
T. Davidson, treasurer
R. Christie, secretary
1903—J. Thomson, president
T. Davidson, treasurer
R. Christie, secretary
1904—J. Thomson, president
R. Christie, secretary and treasurer
1905—J. Thomson, president
R. Christie, secretary
1906—J. Thomson, president
R. Christie, secretary
1907—R. Christie, vice-president
1908—M. Scott, vice-president
1909—R. Christie, vice-president
G. L. McDonald, secretary
1910—R. Christie, vice-president
T. S. Thomson, vice-president
G. L. McDonald, secretary
A. Houliston, treasurer
1911—R. Christie, vice-president
T. S. Thomson, vice-president
A. Houliston, treasurer
1912—T. S. Thomson, vice-president
A. Houliston, treasurer
1913—T. S. Thomson, vice-president
A. Houliston, treasurer
1914—T. S. Thomson, vice-president
A. Houliston, treasurer
1915—T. S. Thomson, vice-president
R. Christie, treasurer
A. J. Grieve, secretary
1920—T. S. Thomson, vice-president
1921—T. S. Thomson, vice-president
1922—T. S. Thomson, vice-president
1923—T. S. Thomson, vice-president
1924—T. S. Thomson, vice-president
1928—W. F. Ellis, treasurer
1929—W. F. Ellis, treasurer

S.B.A.A.A. Officials (continued)

1930—W. F. Ellis, treasurer
1931—W. F. Ellis, treasurer
1932—R. Crawford, vice-president
W. F. Ellis, treasurer
1933—W. F. Ellis, treasurer
1934—W. F. Ellis, treasurer
1935—R. Crawford, president
W. F. Ellis, treasurer
1936—R. Crawford, president
W. F. Ellis, treasurer
1937—R. Crawford, president
W. F. Ellis, treasurer
1938—R. Crawford, president
W. F. Ellis, treasurer
1939—R. Crawford, president
W. F. Ellis, treasurer
1946—R. Crawford, president
W. F. Ellis, treasurer
1947—J. Campbell, treasurer
1948—J. Campbell, treasurer
1949—J. Campbell, treasurer
1950—W. Nichol, treasurer
1951—W. Nichol, treasurer
1952—W. Nichol, treasurer
1953—W. Nichol, treasurer
1954—W. Nichol, treasurer
1955—J. Veitch, treasurer
1956—J. Veitch, treasurer
1965—J. C. Carruthers, vice-president
1967—J. C. Carruthers, president
1968—J. C. Carruthers, president
1969—J. M. Hamilton, vice-president
1971—J. M. Hamilton, president
J. G. S. Smith, vice-president
1972—J. M. Hamilton, president
J. G. S. Smith, vice-president
1973—J. G. S. Smith, president
1974—J. G. S. Smith, president
1977—J. M. Hamilton, president
1978—G. Meikle, president
1980—R. Wilkinson, president
A. Douglas, vice-president
1981—R. Wilkinson, president
1982—R. Wilkinson, president
A. Douglas, vice-president
1983—A. Douglas, president
1984—A. Douglas, president